Poetic Expressions is now Pep T
Publishing. You can contact aut[h
certified professional coach Lorr....
email at Lorraine@PepTalkCAP.com

MW01142710

Lauren,
You are wonderful
and a beautiful
person.
Wishing you
the best
Lorraine
Morgan Scott

PUBLISHER'S NOTE

Except as otherwise noted, this work is the opinions, ideas, and techniques of Lorraine Morgan Scott. When names have been used, they have been changed to protect the individual's privacy, and many stories have been blended to make one. Any resemblance to a specific person, living or dead, is entirely coincidental.

Disclaimer

This self-development book is a single tool in a toolbox of methods and solutions when overcoming events of the past that have shadowed the present and the future. If any stated methods disagree with the advice of professional clinicians or psychological best practices, the reader may be better served by staying with traditional methods. The author is not providing medical advice or medical solutions; she is merely stating opinions and methods that have helped her to achieve balance, inner peace, communication effectiveness, a positive self-image and many of her goals. If you bought this book thinking otherwise, you may return the unread book for a full refund.

The Source Book may be copied by the owner of the book only, or through normal public library use. No other part of this publication may be reproduced in whole or in part, or stored in a retrieval system, or transmitted in any form or by any means, electronic, mechanical, photocopying, recording, or otherwise, without written permission of the publisher. For information regarding permission or to obtain a group-book discount, write: Editor, Poetic Expressions Publishing, PO Box 2367, Springfield, VA 22152, or email PEPPUB@gmail.com.

ISBN: 978-0-9819875-0-7
Library of Congress Catalog Control Number: 2009926634
Printed and bound in the United States
Signature Book Printing, www.sbpbooks.com
1-Self-development, 2-Self-help, 3-Psychology

Contents

This book is for those who have suffered because of another's person's dissatisfaction with them self or life.

May this book help you heal, and help you prevent YOU from continuing the cycle of abuse that was inflicted upon YOU.

Loving Myself First
Overcoming Life's
Obstacles
(Past, Present and Future)

Lorraine Morgan Scott

Poetic Expressions Publishing

PEP talk for your heart and soul ®
Enjoy a book or audio disk today.

Poetic Expressions Publishing
Published by Poetic Expressions Publishing
PO Box 2367, Springfield, CA 22152
PEPPUB@gmail.com

To Mom, May she find the peace that escaped her in life.

I can't believe she's gone
It's like she's only away
I expect to pick up the phone
And ask about her day

Want to see how she is
And see what she's been up to
Want to share the latest news
And things I'm going to do

No I can't believe she's gone
This is gonna take some time
Cause there's a void inside of me
When I realize, yet again, where she used to be

Yes, it's gonna take some time
To stop before I start
Before impulse to pick up the phone
And realizing hurts my heart.

                    With Love, your daughter Lorraine

To you, the reader:

For the guts to pick up this book
For recognizing you want more
Than the hand that life has given you
Or the choices you have made

Life is not a card game
The stakes are so much higher
Yet every day's a gamble
And the jackpot what you make it

So take a look at your hand
And see how it stacks up
You're looking for the royal flush
Preferably in hearts
                    My best to you, Lorraine

Praise for Loving Myself First

"**Well constructed and complete. The language was consistent, readable, and very up-beat.**"
Gary Howard, Ph.D. Bio-Chemistry, Carnegie Mellon University, author and/or editor of 5 books, and dozens of articles.

"**I felt like I could do anything after reading this book.**"
Lisa Yambrick, professional writer and editor

"**Ms. Scott has taken her life experiences and turned them into a step by step motivator for people trying to overcome difficult obstacles. She gives the reader the opportunity to review what is not working for them and implement new ways of thinking and acting. This book also allows the reader time to understand their specific problems and write them down in a workbook for future reference and reflection. Ms. Scott has given the reader a valuable tool for future success.**"
Kathy Anderson, Ph.D., Clinical Psychologist, and Adjunct Faculty Psychology, Los Rios Community College, California

Introduction

Fill your heart with love and self-respect and breathe desire into all things you do. The outcome is astounding.

This book and the exercises in it are designed to be simple and easy to follow, and the methods outlined allow you to get to your life in a positive way.

On the following pages, you'll find techniques to strengthen your inner self and change your current thought processes. Years of different experiences (what I call "learning points") have shaped you into who you are today, your beautiful self. You are beautiful inside and out. Yes, there may be things you don't like, habits you want to change, and qualities you want to improve. To do that, you must first start with self-acceptance. Self-acceptance, self-love, or self-worth allows you to follow the steps to healing, growing, and loving. Accept who you are, where you have been, and where you are going.

It may seem impossible to believe, but I assure you, it is

possible to change your current way of thinking and learn to appreciate who you are "right now." Yes, right now changes daily. That is the beauty of life.

Start making changes in your behavior or your thinking and re-start those dreams. Dreams breathe life into you. Dreams create the urgency to break away from the shackles of a harmful relationship, a destructive environment, poverty, and/or a lack of education.

Are you dreaming of beauty, romance, happiness, good health and prosperity? Do you know it is available to you? It is! Regardless of your background, your current financial position, your current status, your age, your skin color, or your education, all the things mentioned above are possible.

Life's dreams are possible if you believe you can achieve them. They are possible if you take the steps necessary to effect change. Fill your heart with love and self-respect and breathe desire into all things you do. The outcome is astounding and life becomes clearer when you follow and live your dreams.

We all place limits on our self at times. This book will show you how to set new limits, achieve them, and set newer limits still. Understand what is in your mind, what is holding you back, what your strengths are, and what weaknesses you must overcome to achieve your self-awareness, and you will learn how to play the game of life. The result is your life the way you want it, the way you dream about it.

So go on ... dream big. Dream without limits, and when you are ready, and we get to that point in the book, you'll take those dreams and make them into goals. You'll take those goals and make action plans, steps that make a path. With each step on the path you'll reach an objective, and after completing a couple steps you'll have reached a pre-determined milestone; a checkpoint on your journey to a healthier (inside and out) happier, and more fulfilled you.

How do I know this? When I was a young girl, I dreamed of becoming a singer, a songwriter, and an author or storyteller. As I got older and as 'life' threw rocks at me and as I came across learning points, I strayed from dreaming. I did things, saw things, said things, and thought things that weren't in line with good spiritual beliefs or everyday decent morals.

During those years, I was not able to see my inner beauty or my self-worth. I had a lack of self-respect and little confidence. I didn't know how to protect myself from people that would use me, I didn't know how to set boundaries, or respect boundaries set by others. I looked to others to make me feel worthy, attractive, or desirable. Often, almost always, I would be disappointed because I did not receive the things I thought I needed. Others would not fulfill—could not fulfill—what I was missing inside, and I would allow disappointment to ruin my relationships.

When I happened to come across a good person, I didn't know it. I found it difficult to recognize a good friend or a good man when I saw one.

It took a long time, a lot of prayer, and yes, guidance and input from people I met along the way who taught me forgiving myself was the most important start to loving and forgiving others. After learning to forgive my self, I was able to forgive my parents, my siblings, and others who had committed wrongs against me.

You may have also had some learning points in your life. If so, this book is ideal for you. If you recognize some of the traits I've mentioned, then the methods I've developed may help you find your inner beauty, appreciate your outer beauty, build your self-worth, gain confidence, and develop a positive self-image.

I hope you find this book beneficial beyond your expectations. Your feedback is most welcome, as are any questions you may have. Please send them to: lorraine@lovingmyselffirst.com.

Let go of the hate, the fear, the negativity, and drink in compassion, courage, and optimism.

I wish you the best in your journey of self-discovery and self-acceptance, and know life is beautiful when you can love yourself and others.

Many thanks and much love and appreciation are sent to:

Marla Stone, LCSW, of South OC Wellness for her help and guidance in the creation of this book, sharing your "Anger Management," as well as reading my words to ensure I was not steering people in the wrong direction. You have a huge heart, and are adept at getting to the root of the issue. I wish you the greatest success with your 'practice'.

Dr. Gary Howard. I appreciate your time and recommendations regarding my manuscript, and I cherish your "man's" review of the book because the book was written primarily for women.

Okneco McTier, for pushing me to be better without even realizing you were doing it.

My husband, Ken, and son Nathan, who lost me to my writing and research for many, many, many and even many more hours while I mentally re-lived my past. Yes Ken, now that I believe in myself, it'll be hard to keep my feet on the ground as I soar to reach my dreams. You are welcome to borrow my rose-colored glasses anytime. Thanks for your love and support through all these years of self-discovery. Nathan, I thank you for always supporting me, unconditionally, and I am so delighted you have grown into such a wonderful young man. You have so much potential, I hope you remember to dream and envision your success. You do me and your father proud. And to Jessica, who has, in her own way, caused me to grow and become more compassionate. You *can* achieve what is buried in your heart.

My beautiful first born, Stephanie, who has had to experience much of my pain, my joys, my struggles, my insecurities, and continually share me and her life with more and more people. Stephanie, you've watched as I've grown to who I am today with always an encouraging word on your lips. I am so very proud of you and your accomplishments and your determination, and the goodness you possess. I am so thankful you have become such a beautiful person inside and out. Your successes are yours because you worked hard for them—you are terrific.

I thank God for giving me the ability to write what I'm thinking, and the strength to put it into words. I feel so fortunate to have you. The learning points I've experienced were not in vain. I have so much to give to others because of the events in my life, and I thank you, Lord, for the ability to learn, continually, and not remain in the past.

And lastly, to the reader, I thank you for looking inward, outward, and forward. Life is tough sometimes, and when we can share what we've learned to help others, it often makes things a little bit easier, a little bit brighter. Hopefully, you'll be able to share the knowledge and insights you receive here and brighten someone else's day.

Should you find this book whet's an appetite to further your development beyond the parameters of this book, the type of professional assistance you may find helpful (if you liked what I've said here) would be a psychologist who uses the cognitive perspective of learning. This means they'll help you take what you've learned (through this book or through session) and make changes in your behavior.

9

On, March 8, 2009, in honor of International Women's Day, U.S. Secretary of State Hillary Clinton, released a press statement so in tune with the objective of this book I felt I needed to include it here. I've summarized, but you can find it on the web at www.state.gov, look under press releases, March 2009.

Secretary Clinton wrote, "...honor women around the world who are blazing trails and surmounting obstacles in pursuit of equality and opportunity. Although you may not know their names or recognize their faces, these women advocates are hard at work in every country and on every continent, seeking to fulfill their right to participate fully in the political, economic and cultural lives of their societies. Often working against great odds and at great personal sacrifice, they are a key to global progress in this new century and deserve our admiration and support."

She adds the importance of including women in "addressing the complex challenges we face in this new century, whether it be the economic crisis, the spread of terrorism, regional conflicts that threaten families and communities, we will not solve these challenges through half measures. Yet too often, on these issues half the world is left behind. No nation in the world has yet achieved full equality for women. Women still comprise the majority of the world's poor, unfed, and unschooled. They are subjected to physical, sexual, and psychological violence and subjection. Like all people, women deserve to live free from violence and fear."

Adding Secretary Clinton's speech is not an endorsement of this book by her or the State Department. It's included to demonstrate how personal acceptance, self-confidence, and self-love are factors that allow you to champion the needs of others. It is these characteristics that provide the necessary internal support to aid others, provide love and even empathy. We all grow exponentially when we help others.

10

1:
Assessing Who We Are

We begin this book at the beginning. How are you today? What is going right? What part of you do you want to delve deeper into to find out what makes you happy, sad, angry, or hurt?

We begin with an assessment that will ask some interesting questions. Answer quickly, and write the first answer that comes to mind.

Isn't it amazing that often, we may try to cheat ourselves and write what we *think* looks good, not what is real, even though no one can see what we wrote. Answer these questions immediately without thinking. How else can you discover what is really in your mind?

If you spend too much time on a question, your mind will take over and tell you something different, something you may want to see written down.

We (well, you) want your original thinking and not a contrived response. This book is a journey. It will take you deep into soul-searching, ask you to ask yourself some questions, and then look at those answers with a mind willing to change. You may want to keep a notepad and pencil handy for all the ideas you'll generate. That way you can refer back to them as your journey unfolds. Additionally, when you see the pencil image, that means you have the opportunity to answer questions, write down ideas, or elaborate on possible sources of reasons you feel the way you do in the accompanying Source Book. The Source Book is designed in such a way that you can easily copy the pages, then cut them along the dotted line, and then clip or staple the pages together so they can be carried with you easily.

It may sound silly, but you may enjoy coloring the borders of your Source Book, thus adding personality, inspiration and flair to the pages of YOU—past, present, and future.

The recommendations I make come from surviving "learning points", as well as some from notable authors, psychologists, and psychiatrists. I highlight what I believe are the nine areas making up a balanced, happy you. I hope you'll agree that strengthening each of these characteristics bring you joy, balance, and an improved sense of self.

Although I am not a mental health professional, I am an expert on survival. I am a wife (of years in double digits), a mother (of a teenaged boy and an adult daughter), a step-mother of an adult daughter who lived with us for 13 years, a daughter, and a survivor of abusive relationships that began in childhood. The difficulties that accompanied the joys, as well as the coping skills life teaches, have led to this book.

I have "been there, done that, and lived to tell the tale." I write this book to benefit you. I also use the methods written here in my workshops and seminars. My Beauty Seminars mantra is *Dream, Believe, Visualize, Achieve*™.

So, let's begin your journey.

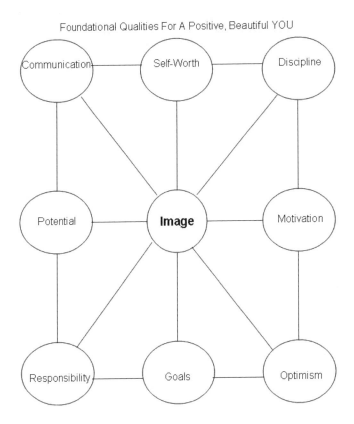

Foundational Qualities For A Positive, Beautiful YOU

Do you see how each of these attributes or characteristics are related and inter-related to each other, but that each of them is attached to the self-image?

It is difficult to be one, or have one, without the other. If you are not optimistic, how motivated do you think you'll be? Or if you don't see your potential, how can you set goals? If you lack the discipline to set goals, regardless of your motivation level, you'll wander aimlessly because you don't have a path to follow or guide you. Do you agree or disagree?

13

Today's Assessment

1. Do you **often** wish you were **someone** else? **Y N**

2. Do you **often** wish you were thinner or heavier? **Y N**

3. Do you wish to significantly change your appearance as in be taller/shorter, different nose, chin, etc? **Y N**

4. Are you a compulsive volunteer (Can't say no)? **Y N**

5. When praised, do you say "yeah right" or laugh? **Y N**

6. When asked what makes you happy do you have to think about it? **Y N**

7. Is "I'm not sure," your answer when asked about your goals? **Y N**

8. Do you think you have to be outwardly beautiful or rich to get what you want? **Y N**

9. Is being unique or different a bad thing? **Y N**

10. Do you **often** say "I can't, I have to, or I should?" **Y N**

11. Do you make a daily "to-do" list, but still don't seem to complete anything? **Y N**

12. When you make a mistake, do you call yourself a name, such as Dummy, Stupid, or Idiot? **Y N**

13. Do you NOT make a suggestion or NOT try something new because you are afraid to fail or be laughed at? **Y N**

14. Do you believe your mate, a pretty face, or an education is responsible for your happiness? **Y N**

15. If opportunity knocked, would you feel you weren't quite ready? **Y N**

Use the non-scientific scoring suggestions on the next page to see how you'll benefit from this book.

Scoring Guidelines for the Personal Assessment

If you circled No 9–12 times you may be:
- Getting manipulated by others
- Putting the needs of others before yourself
- Saying 'yes' instead of 'no' too often

If you circled No 6–8 times you may be:
- Suffering from depression
- Missing the significance in tasks and daily living
- Yo-yo dieting
- Following fads or celebrities in an unhealthy manner

If you circled No 2–5 times you may be:
- Having a hard time finding happiness
- Suffering from depression
- Un-accepting of your self in any manner
- Allowing others to direct your activities

If you have circled No 2–5 times, please read this book in its entirety, and then go back and do the each exercise. If, while reading the book or doing the exercises in the Source Book, or thoughts' surfacing during any of the discovery process makes you feel threatened or more depressed, please seek professional psychiatric or psychological counseling as soon as you can.

If you scored 6–15 No's, this book will be ideal in pinpointing issues and challenges you may presently face.

Save your assessment and let's start this journey. Be excited ... I am for you.

"A successful person is one who can lay a firm foundation with the bricks that others throw at him."
David Brink

"Life is a field of unlimited possibilities."
Deepak Chopra

2: Our Self-Image

Self-image. Why is it so important? What is self-image? Well, Webster defines self-image as one's conception of oneself or of one's role. But what does that mean?

Basically, it means that our self-image is formed by who or what **we think** we are. We determine it. Isn't that great news? It is. That means we can change our self-image. We can change how we perceive *our* self. We can change how we view *our* role. What a great feeling it is to know we are in charge of our own self-image.

The sad part for many of us, though, is that we allow others to shape, change, affect, lower, and ruin __our__ self-image. We give them that power!

You can take back that power!
You can determine your own self-image.
You have the right to determine what your role is in your life.

We listen to what they say. If someone criticizes us or puts us down and we (even mentally) don't dispute what was said,

17

we absorb the negative words like butter on toast. So what happens to the absorbed negativity? It builds and builds and our foundation becomes one of self-loathing instead of one of self-love.

If you've had a poor self-image for a while or have had people putting you down and making you feel bad about yourself, it will take some time and a lot of conscious effort to change your way of thinking. Don't believe me? Do you think that what someone (or lots of someones) has said has no bearing on how you perceive yourself? It does – a lot.

Let me give you an example. Susan Wilson Solovic, author of *The Girl's Guide to Building a Million-Dollar Business*, and *The Girl's Guide to Power and Success*, was basically told she was "mentally challenged" because she scored low on the sixth grade standardized test. While all her friends were placed in accelerated classes, Susan, who had what amounted to test anxiety, was placed in a class for mentally challenged students. It wasn't until four years later, when Susan was in the tenth grade, that a caring counselor provided the right encouragement to help her realize her potential.

This shows how *even one incident* (a principal using one method of evaluation) can change a young child who had previously earned excellent grades into a child with a negative self-perception.

She had absorbed the negative image others had of her. After hearing something so often, you expect it even it isn't there. Do you know what I mean?

You probably read *even **when** it isn't there*, and it (when) wasn't, or maybe you read and thought: *even **if** it isn't there,* and (if) wasn't.

It is human nature (and our knowledge of syntax) to fill in the blanks, to complete the sentence. If you are used to hearing you're dumb, ugly, stupid, nasty, so forth, and hearing it becomes commonplace, you have absorbed it, and it has affected your self image.

> *If someone you loved or respected has told you repeatedly that you are ugly and unworthy, how likely do you think it is that you could look in the mirror and see your beauty, whether your inner beauty or your outer beauty. I'd say unlikely.*

Often, name calling comes from a mean, vindictive person who has used you as a means of escaping her own sadness, sorrow, or personal torture and wants to make you feel bad about your self-image, so she can rise above you. Other times, such verbal abuse comes from a person who had been the receiver of the same emotional trauma(s), and is repeating the parenting model or methods used against her.

You may be receiving what she did when she was your age and she sees no reason to deviate from the way she was raised or treated.

That's the hard part, figuring out where it all went wrong, the "it" being why you were treated (or are being treated) like that in the first place. Some people think, "So what, get over it. It doesn't matter *why* she said or did what she did."

I disagree, but we'll get more into that later. Back to you and your difficult identification of cause.

Let's say you understand or agree that you may have some issues that have affected your self-image or how you feel about yourself. And let's say you've had these thoughts for a while (or 5-20 years) and don't see how you can shake or change them.

I'm going to show you. You **can** change the way you think, you can change the way you see yourself, and you **can** change the way you feel about yourself. You only have to "trick" your brain and change your thought process.

This book may have reached your hands after you've received years of negative input, and you might be wondering if it isn't already too late. It isn't! You can change your thinking and start getting and giving positive input, one word, or one thought process at a time. It's exciting.

2:2 Your Thought Process

Your brain is magnificent. It has unlimited capability and capacity. Really. You'll spend your whole life learning and still not fill it up. I've heard that most people use 3–5 percent of their brain capability, how is that for over-achievers. To change your thought process, you'll be expanding on that 3 percent, but first let's look at what changing your thought process entails.

Each person has basically three levels of thoughts. They are kind of like layers in the earth or, in technical terms, a computer system. As much as I love my HP, it will never compare to the brain's capability or capacity.

Through the brain you have conscious thoughts, subconscious thoughts, and unconscious thoughts. Together, your thought processes work in steps.

Your senses take information in. These are initial, conscious judge-like senses: warm, hot, happy, angry, pretty, and so forth.

Your conscious passes these thoughts to the subconscious, which is a nonjudgmental recorder of information.

From there, your subconscious passes it to your unconscious for storage. Picture a computer. The screen would be the conscious, the auto-save to "my documents" would be the subconscious, and the "C" drive, trashcan, or the place that keeps a record of everything you've ever done on your computer like the "dos" is the unconscious.

 Here is a visual of the process:

Action: You are sitting on a park bench watching the birds. A dog races past the bench, bumps your leg, and barks loudly as it is running after the birds. Your conscious mind receives the information, makes any judgmental thoughts about what the dog is doing and sends it on its way to the subconscious mind. From there, the subconscious mind processes the

thoughts (e.g., *irresponsible pet owner, great looking dog, ooh, fantastic-looking man running after barking dog ...) and then sends all those thoughts to the unconscious mind.*

As you wait for your friend to join you, you close your eyes. The fantastic-looking man appears and tells you how lovely you look with the sun highlighting your hair. He apologizes for his wayward dog and asks if he can make it up to you over dinner. Of course, you accept.

Then your girlfriend sits down beside you. You chat about this and that and then a dog runs by. Your "conscious thought process" remembers the other dog and sends a message to the unconscious. "Retrieve the story about the dog and its owner," it tells the subconscious. The subconscious responds and brings up the story to the conscious mind.

Excitedly, your memory is jarred and you can tell her about the dog, the fantastic-looking man and ...the dinner date (was it real?)

The same process happens when you dream. Real or fantasy, the subconscious doesn't know the difference.

21

Repetition is the key.

Your conscious is called "judge-like" because it has a label or category for everything that it sees, smells, touches, hears, and tastes. An emotion is usually tied to each of those sensory images.

If you walk outside and a blast of hot humid air makes your glasses fog up immediately (then you know you're in Florida—just kidding), your conscious thought process would be the heat, the wetness, the fogging of your glasses, and the clamminess of your skin.

Realize all of this sensory detail is instantaneous and without your telling yourself to take in these senses. Your conscious thought process judges the weather without any conscious input on your part. Here is where it can become scary and skewed.

If you have never had this happen before, (your glasses fogging up) you record the details: hot air, foggy glasses, and clammy skin.

Your conscious takes it in and transfers it to your subconscious, without any additional input from you. Later on, you find out that the reason your glasses fogged up and your skin felt clammy is because of something called humidity, which is hot air mixed with moisture. When you learn the reason, it is filed away and attached to the sensory details (of the glasses fogging, the clammy skin) which were already filed.

Now, in your subconscious you have a file heading of humidity with the sensory details of hot air, foggy glasses, and clammy skin. None of this was a conscious effort on your part. Your subconscious works your consciousness smoothly.

Your subconscious acts like a computer that has automatic updates and upgrades. It records everything without knowledge of accuracy or reality. Kind of like a tape recorder or the word processing of a fiction writer. Whatever is said is tucked away.

Another way to explain the process is described by Anita Woolfolk in her book *Educational Psychology*. She labels the memory processes sensory, working, and long-term memory. Sensory memory (which is the conscious memory mentioned earlier) is the stimuli, everything seen, heard, smelled, touched, or tasted.

The capacity for sensory memory is extreme, more than you could actually take in all at the same time (kind of like trying to see each event happening in a three-ring circus simultaneously.) Sensory memory only lasts for 1 to 3 seconds.

For the stimuli to remain longer requires the mind to recognize the stimuli and assign it meaning. Woolfolk calls this *perception*, which she explains as "meaning constructed based on both physical representation [the original stimuli] and what your existing [or prior] knowledge is" (pg 251).

In her book, Woolfolk uses a great example to explain what perception is by use of the capital letter "A." Using prior knowledge of the shape of an 'A' (which is stored in long-term memory), we can usually figure out the 'A' written in different fonts and even in someone else's messy writing. A A A A 𝓐 A A A 𝓐 ᴀ See what I mean.

2:3 Retrieving from Your Long-Term Memory

How do we retrieve something from our long-term

memory? Your sensory memory has an enabler, a process that works in conjunction with the memory. This enabler, according to Woolfolk, is knowledge and expectations. It enables you to combine your knowledge of a situation with your knowledge of how your environment works (rules and culture and prior events) and information stored in your memory to analyze the pattern or stimuli before you.

Once you recognize a pattern or stimulus, it is moved to working memory. Working memory has also been called short-term memory or consciousness. Working memory is limited, just a string of words or a few numbers. It is the processor and file clerk for all the new sensory information you have just received. It combines your new information with what you already know and moves it to long-term memory.

This could be bad or good. Good if you grew up with or were otherwise surrounded in a warm and loving environment that was supportive and united. Bad if you were surrounded by, or grew up with unsupportive, mean, harmful, or otherwise damaging individuals.

Here's an example of how incoming stimuli connects with a recognized pattern that was filed in long-term memory.

Say when you were younger, every Friday night your dad stopped off at the neighborhood pub and got drunk. When he came home, he was belligerent and mean. He would strike without provocation, usually at your mom. You witnessed this repeatedly and learned to become invisible at those times.

Years later, in a relationship of your own, the first time your mate got drunk, you became invisible. Your memory coupled with expectation prepared you for what would come next EVEN if your mate behaved nothing like your dad.

This would occur each time your mate got drunk. It wouldn't change until you replaced your old memories (dad +

alcohol = abuse) with new memories *(mate + alcohol = happy drunk)*. *Realistically though, it would be difficult to get to the point that you would be okay being around your mate while he is drinking.*

Although you can change how you perceive yourself (it is no easy feat), it is difficult to change how you perceive a bad memory and another person. Information in your working memory only stays there for about 20 seconds (unless you repeat it over and over again). Long-term memory is categorized into "explicit and implicit," according to Peter Gray in his book *Psychology*.

When you are remembering memories from 10 years ago, last week, or yesterday, you are retrieving long-term memory. The explicit part of the long-term memory is your experiences (episodic) and semantics (facts and general knowledge you've accumulated), and the implicit memory is stuff you do unconsciously or without having to think about each step.

2:4 Priming

This unconscious, implicit memory involves classical conditioning (drunkenness = abuse), procedural memory (how to ride a bike, rules of the road, and school etiquette), and priming (something associated with another thought or event that gives you a base to prepare you for something).

Here is an example of priming. It's a Friday night. An alcohol commercial appears on the television screen. Something alerts you and says, "Wake up. You need to listen or pay attention."

Remember in school when your teacher cleared her throat, stomped her foot, or had some other signal to indicate she were about to say something really important and you needed to listen. That's priming.

Priming is also when someone talks about something or introduces something in a specific manner. Example: *"Richard darling, I had one of those éclairs from Conrad's and my mouth exploded in a symphony of sensation. Tell me. What do you think?"*

Richard (or anyone) would answer that question after first considering what the speaker just said, how he felt about the speaker, and how he felt about the subject. Richard may have thought Conrad's éclair was so-so. But if he respected, liked, or wanted to side with the speaker, he'd probably say, "They were scrumptious." But if he didn't care for the speaker, he might say, "Eh, they were alright, but nothing worth bragging about."

The priming could have a negative or a positive result, depending upon the audience. Another example is this. You were getting dressed in the morning. Your mate (or someone else whose opinion you value) walks in and says, "You're not going to wear that dreadful thing are you? Don't you have something different you can wear?"

You wear it anyway, but your nerves are brittle because of the comments. Other "little" things happen because you're bristling, and then you get to work and hear, "That blouse is unacceptable," or "And why are you wearing that? It's like … UGLY!"

The result is your going off on the last person who gave you her opinion, primarily because you were primed.

2:5 Memory and Priming

Why are priming and the realization you've been primed important? What does all this mean to your self-image? Why is understanding implicit and explicit long-term memory, working memory, unconscious, subconscious, and conscious thoughts and memory so important?

It's important because the past is what brought you to where you are today and to whom you are today. Your past encompasses everything (real or imagined) that you've seen, heard, felt, or thought.

Heard with enough repetition, even a far-out thought can be considered reality. It's like learning the multiplication tables. If you were taught that 3x3 equals 2, that's what you would believe. It would take new learning, through repetition to change your thought process to believe 3x3 equals 9.

What does that mean? It means you could be walking around thinking you're fat, ugly, worthless, non-deserving, stupid, or a host of other unrealistic characters and characteristics.

A good example of a skewed subconscious (or someone who has been fed a line a crap for so long she thinks it is the truth) is someone who suffers from anorexia. Anorexia is an eating disorder (a disease of the mind) that can be life-threatening (you could die from it).

If your subconscious believes you are fat, when you look in the mirror and see your 86-pound body on a five-foot-five frame you are going to see a fat person.

Your conscious checks your subconscious before doing anything or thinking anything. Your eyes may see your skin and bones, but your subconscious is telling your conscious that you are fat. How could this be?

Somewhere, somehow, this person suffering from anorexia was taught he or she was fat and that being fat was a bad thing. It may have happened in the early stages of her life when:

- She had some fat or baby-fat
- She may have heard over and over again: "Oh look, she was so cute and fat. What an adorable baby she was."

- Or, "Look at those chubby cheeks and those chubby legs. Mildred, you were such a fat little girl."
- Worse: "Look at your tummy. Look how it sticks out. You *are* fat!"
- And the self-worth killer: "No one will love you if you're fat."

To hear these comments with fragile ears and an unsure heart is devastating. For someone who is not confident of her looks or confident of her worth, this type of talk can be damaging to her overall self-image. If heard enough times (or even once in an unsure mind), it will be believed as real. And if the person speaking has power over the listener (such as a parent, teacher, or coach), it's regarded as true!

Add unrealistic pictures of skinny girls modeling fashions, celebrities doing everything they can to get the "perfect" body, and dating or relationships, and whew, you have a mess.

If you were the person suffering from anorexia, how could you change this? To change what is being input, you would change what your conscious is receiving.

First, let me add a note of caution here. If you (or someone you know) suffer from severe depression or a life-threatening disease such as anorexia, alcoholism, drug-abuse, bulimia, or if you hear voices in your head telling you to commit acts of violence, get professional help from trained doctors and licensed psychologists.

The issues stated above can be life-threatening because they cause one to do things (in excess) one wouldn't normally do. It isn't difficult to fall into the trap of easing the pain with some mind-altering substance. And without a strong sense of worth and confidence, it isn't difficult to fall in the trap of extreme dieting.

This book can help you on your journey to overcoming the

obstacles in your past, present, and future, but if you're suffering these illnesses, please seek professional help.

Okay, now back to changing what your conscious is receiving. What are you feeding your consciousness? What stimuli is your sensory memory taking in and passing to your long-term memory?

Here is an exercise for you. Open your Source Book to 2-1. Close your eyes. Take a few moments to replay your day in your mind. What happened today? What did you see, do, feel, or hear? Now, in your Source Book, write down everything you can think about your day. Don't think. Just write.

When finished, ask yourself, what didn't you include about your day? Did you include the following in your writing?

- Positive thoughts or happy events
- Things that made you happy or feel good
- Little actions (a hug), words (thank you), or images (someone smiling) that brightened your day?

We have a tendency to both look at the big picture when asked a question such as that, and to minimize the situation. We also have a tendency to look at things negatively.

If you were primed for the question, you might have included such things as:

I woke early this morning. As I sipped my coffee, I listened to the birds singing and chattering, and watched as they flew around the trees outside excitedly. My morning ran smoothly with only a couple of snags getting the kids ready for school. Michael was very angry over a misplaced sweater, but Natalie had a great smile and a big hug for me. Traffic stunk as usual. I spent my time listening to a language tape so got in a few extra minutes of practice.

At work, it was one crisis after another. The copier broke down when I needed it most. I could have screamed in anguish. I hit my head (really hard) on an open cabinet, and I realized I had forgotten my lunch.

As I sat there steaming, Michelle (a coworker) dropped off a goofy-looking smiley-face sticker and a lunch invitation. The copy machine was fixed and cleaned, and not by me.

My son called and apologized for his earlier anger and told me he loved me.

Your present self-image has a lot to do with what you think about when you are reflecting on something or asked to think about a specific thing or event. Remember that little thing called perception?

If your present self-image is a negative one, or you are used to thinking negative thoughts, or you're always tired, hurried, late, angry, or continually around negative people, negativity will be your dominate thought. How could it not? You'll see the negativity in each situation, and you'll expect bad things to happen.

On the other hand, if you are a positive person, upbeat, cheerful, and full of energy, I would expect that your review of your day would have that rosy outlook as well. You are the type that attracts other happy, cheerful people. I'm sure you've heard that like attracts like. Even in a negative situation, you know something good that can come from it.

What the exercise should show is this. Your brain processes sensory details through three levels: conscious, subconscious, and unconscious (or sensory, working, and long-term). At what level you process depends upon your present state.

Many people sleep while playing a CD with nature sounds or soothing music to relax the subconscious or play a tape recorder with a language or school subject review (such as biology notes) to learn.

2:6 Unconscious Thoughts

Even when you are unconscious or sleeping or not consciously listening, your brain can receive input. Have you ever caught yourself able to repeat a conversation you weren't consciously listening to? Crazy, huh?

Many times our brain is processing stuff, and we don't even realize it. Dr. Waitley, a psychologist, personifies it as your "robot self-image." Your robot records, but it doesn't know and can't distinguish from imagination or reality. If someone is constantly telling you that you are worthless, stupid, a failure, or a loser, your robot self-image is recording all this. You may think you aren't listening, but you are. You are even recording it.

It won't be long until that is what you feel about yourself. No way, you say? Think back to the assessment you did earlier and ask yourself the following questions.

- When you stub your toe, do you call yourself a name, like *idiot*? As in "You're such an idiot."
- When there is a problem, do you immediately get angry at the other person before finding out and listening to the whole story?
- Do you disregard someone else's thoughts or feelings because they don't match yours?
- Are you afraid to approach someone you like because you think you aren't good enough?
- Do you hide in the back row so you aren't noticed or called upon?
- When someone tells you you're beautiful or that you look good, do you accept it as truth, or is there self-doubt?
- If you're making a call to ask something from someone,

31

do you hesitate?
- When asked to tell something about yourself do you stammer, not wanting to "brag?"
- If you have accomplished something, and someone congratulates you on it, do you minimize the accomplishment and say, "It was nothing."

2:7 Learned Behaviors

Answers to the above questions are affected by your self-image. Are you putting yourself down, defensive, close-minded, trying to become invisible, or are you not able to promote yourself? All of these negative thoughts and self put-downs come from our self-image. The good news is that your negative self-image was learned and developed. You weren't born with any negative qualities, or negative thoughts, or a negative self-image. You developed it over time.

At the top of the next page is a (by no means all-inclusive) list of some *learned behaviors.*

Fears	Copying	Anxieties
Low self-esteem	Antagonistic	Self-doubt
Self-pity	Low standards	Aggressiveness
Steadfastness	High standards	Language
Etiquette	Ridiculing others	Valor
Integrity	Honesty	Dishonesty
Guilt	Embarrassment	Inadequacy
Poor judgment	Destructiveness	Confidence
Selfishness	Capability	Courage
Commitment	Compassion	Creativity

Do you notice from the short list above that there are always two ends to the pendulum? There are low standards ←-----------------→ and high standards and the standards you have may be somewhere in between. The funny thing about standards is that they can change to rise or fall depending on your expectations.

In the army, we have minimum standards on many tests. One is the physical fitness test. To meet the minimum standard, a service member must do a certain number of pushups and sit ups and must run 2 miles in a specified time. If someone fails to meet the standard, and the scorer "gives 'em one," then a new standard has been set. It is a lower standard and one without integrity, but a new standard nonetheless.

Another example is customer service. If a company expects you to answer the phone within three rings, and you make it a point to answer in two rings, you have set a new standard, a higher standard, but a new standard nonetheless.

The point is to show you that they are **learned behaviors**. Maybe you have a low self-image at this time. Maybe it's because you don't have a strong foundation of learned behaviors to draw upon. Let me tell you a true (and recent from 2008) story.

As I was preparing for a teaching position, I was reading books to familiarize myself with the content my students would be reading, as well as the types of material I would be reading aloud.

After each short story, my heart zinged. How I wish I had been that parent to my children. How I wish I had that imagination or experience from which to draw from as a writer. How I wish I had had those experiences as a child.

As I felt the ineffectiveness of my parenting deep within, I stopped. I changed my thought process. Here I was beating myself up because I didn't have imagination like A. Cameron, and because I wasn't that fabulous and inventive parent

highlighted in the book, The Stories Julian Tells *(a series).
How could I?*

*Such kindness, such support, such imagination, and such
love **are learned behaviors**. Those characteristics weren't
shown to me when I was a child, so I was never afforded the
opportunity to learn them. I've got to stop beating myself up
for what I wasn't and congratulate myself on the things I
have accomplished, on the cycles I have broken.*

*My ancestor's cycles include abuse from both of my parents,
alcoholism by both of my parents, smoking by both parents
and grandparents, and lack of education by both parents and
some of my grandparents to name a few. I broke the cycle. I
refused to be like them. **I chose to learn new behaviors
and not mimic those used against me**.*

*I don't abuse my children, or alcohol, or smoke (any more),
and I am dedicated to furthering my education. I have
demonstrated qualities I would like to have my children mimic
(yet sadly, some I hope they don't as well). I changed my
learned behaviors for the better, the more supportive, and
more loving. Hopefully, these are the ones they'll mimic. But
before I could do that, I had to learn what they were {the
bad ones} and how to change them. **This is how and why
this book came about**.*

The following ***learned thought processes*** (and additional
ones not shown) can be changed from negative thoughts to
positive thoughts with a little effort.

<u>Negative</u>	<u>Positive</u>
Trapped	Resourceful
Desperate	Potential
Inadequate	Creative
Drowning	Energized
Rock bottom	Competent
Destructive	Positive

Negative	**Positive**
Anxious	Meaningful
Negative	Accomplished
Burdened	Balanced
Overwhelmed	Excited
Frustrated	Harmonized
Depressed	Capable
Resentful	Joyful
Insecure	Confident
Intimidated	Exuberant
Unworthy	Committed
Insufficient	Courageous
Unable	Successful
Unlovable	Loveable
Unattractive	Attractive
Unacknowledged	Recognized

If you feel you have qualities you want to change, you can. You can, over time, learn to have a positive self image, a positive mind-set, and a positive state of mind. It isn't difficult to change your thought process, but it isn't easy either.

To change your self-image you must first improve those foundational qualities you looked at earlier. To change or improve upon those qualities, you will need to change your subconscious thoughts.

On the following pages are techniques for changing your thought processes. You'll identify what those thoughts are; the good, the bad, and the in-between. The techniques I recommend to change your thought process may take time to internalize, but after consistent use, you'll find yourself thinking more positively and treating yourself better. You'll be amazed at your improved self-image.

You want to be able to STOP the negative thoughts immediately as I did when I was reading those short stories.

To do that requires knowing what you do well, knowing what you have accomplished, and knowing what makes you proud about yourself. This knowledge is essential for combating negativity.

Make multiple copies of the Source Book pages so you can do the exercises today and then again after you've had time to let what you've learned take effect.

Here's one more thing about negative thoughts. They multiply. Have you ever noticed that if you're feeling angry or negative about something, if those feelings are allowed to fester, you'll find your self engulfed with negativity. Nip it as soon as you realize you have it!

2:8 Your Thoughts Identified

In your Source Book, make a list of every negative thought you have about yourself. Yes, every thought, regardless of how small. Write freely.

Next, write down positive thoughts you have about yourself. Again, write every thought, regardless of how small.

And now, what are those in-between thoughts? Sometimes they're negative and sometimes they're positive (or almost positive.) These would be actions or ideas you exhibit like a leaf blowing in the wind. *As an example of this difficult-to-identify thought, I share my inconsistency of consideration for others. Sometimes I am considerate, compassionate, and courteous, while other times, I can be down right mean. I let my environment affect my thought process and I become something I don't want to be.*

After you've identified (and exposed) those thoughts to the light (and your consciousness), try writing down the positive attribute of those negative or in between thoughts. For example, if you wrote:

36

Negative		**Positive**
Short Fused	the positive is	*Thinks Before Acting*
Inconsiderate	the positive is	*Considerate*

After thinking of the positive attributes, you'd write down two or three ways you can practice to internalize those qualities. Here are some **examples** for those written above:

Short-fused. Instead of immediately lashing out in anger:
- Put yourself in a time-out, or
- Count to 10 or 20 slowly, or
- See if there is more to the story, or
- Find out all the facts before reacting.

Inconsiderate. Becoming (or being) considerate takes forethought. If your normal action is to do for yourself first, catch yourself. Make the effort to ask if someone needs something when you're getting up or going out. Pass the platter without taking one first. Do a good deed without be asked.

2:9 Change Your Learned Process

Did you think of some positive thoughts or attributes to replace the in-between or negative ones? If not, re-look at your notes. What are some ways you can change your learned process and behavior to act and react how you'd prefer to be? How do you want to be? It's your drawing board. It's your blank canvas. If you need help, ask someone what they would do, or how they would do it.

What about qualities or attributes we don't have, but that we admire. Are there any you'd like to possess? Would you like to be more accepting of yourself and others? Would you like more patience? How is your detachment? Are you too concerned with what other people think? Are you judgmental?

When we are honest about our qualities, we'll find we

~ Lorraine Morgan Scott ~

need to improve on some, but on others we need to set some boundaries. An example of setting some boundaries is with our time or resources.

We may find we are the "go to" person all the time. Our time is monopolized because we stop and help, take over a task, or have a problem saying no. Clear boundaries and respect for our time (and resources) improves our environment. So helpfulness may be a quality we possess, but one we need to have control over or restraint with.

In your Source Book, write the qualities (or virtues) you don't have or have in short supply. Some examples are purposefulness, assertiveness, commitment, diligence, determination, perseverance, patience, and idealism.

And you guessed it, now write an action plan to learn and develop those qualities so they become a true part of YOU. Don't know how to write an action plan? Read on.

There's nothing to dread about planning. Writing a plan lets you see what steps you should take next and what is next expected.

2:10 Your Physical Characteristics

Up until now, you've written personal qualities, attributes, or characteristics that you have or would like to possess. Now you are going to take a good look at the physical part of you.

In your Source Book, write down what you like or dislike about the physical characteristics that make up you. Start by writing down what you **Like and Dislike.** Write down qualities you can learn (in time) to accept (qualities you aren't able to change).

Look at the list. If your dislike list is longer than your like list, you need to look deeper. Maybe you like how your eye

38

lashes curl or your lungs don't give out after ascending 10 stairs.

After you have your list, look especially at what you put on your *dislike* list. Decide what you can change and what can't you change. If you have dislikes about your body* (see next page) that are nearly impossible to change or that your financial status doesn't support, try looking for ways you can change your thinking.

In your Source Book, write a letter to yourself and explain how those dislikes can be changed to acceptance. Be gracious. There is not one perfect person in this world. Why challenge yourself to be the first one? When you have finished your letter, review it.

It is easier to change how you perceive something, then to constantly rethink it or worry about it. An example is if you are 5'1" tall, and you would prefer to be 5'6". You can constantly wear heels, but that can be painful on your back and posture, and you probably wouldn't wear platforms or heels with 5 inches.

It would be more beneficial to your sanity if you learned to accept your height. Ways to do this could be to find role models of the same height or to wear clothes that make you appear taller or clothes that accentuate another part of your body you do feel good about (like your legs.) Or, even better, think of reasons why 5'1" is a good height to be. Daily, reinforce your thinking, and soon you'll be able to accept your height positively.

To recap, asking your self all these questions is the basis for your action plan. You've identified your likes and dislikes, identified what you are unable to change, and written a letter to yourself seeking self-acceptance. Have you identified your wonderful qualities that overshadow that scar or those spider veins? Your mind will accept what you feed it, so now you'll determine nutritious ingredients to start the change.

The more positive food (and thoughts) you ingest, the happier (and healthier) your mind, heart, and body will be. So write those ugly thoughts away and review your positive thoughts daily.

* If you are considering changing your body through surgery, I ask that you look at the reasons first. It you feel the change is the only way you'll be attractive, or you are doing it so someone else is pleased – your mind isn't in the right place. What I mean by this is, if your whole self-confidence is based upon this one thing – the change isn't going to fulfill your needs. You'll immediately find something else that needs to be changed. Say you don't like your chin, so you get it sculpted. Now your nose no longer fits your face, so you get that changed. Wow, that straight nose really shows off the sag in your eyes.

On the other hand, if you were happy with all aspects of your face (you probably wouldn't need the chin changed) except did not really care for the strong chin – you may have different results. You may feel the change portrays the softer you, the nurturing you, the "you" that wasn't projected with the strong chin.

2:11 Setting Change in Motion

The first and easiest step in making a change is (and you may have heard of them) to use affirmations. Affirmations are statements that assert the truth or existence of something. They may be something you want to become true. Critical elements of affirmations (also called self-talk) are:

• Write and say them in the present. "I am or I have"
• Read and say them every day, preferably multiple times each day.
• Include what you are grateful for.

- Even though they may not be true (yet) and you may not believe them (yet), have faith.

After you've written out affirmations and placed them where you'll see them (for reminding), let your mind and your pencil wander.

Let's say one quality you would like to possess or expand is patience. This is a virtue most of us need more of, so it's a good guess that you might have written it down. How could one get more patience?

First, what is it? How many times has someone told you to be something or do something and you didn't know what it was? Have you ever told a child to "be patient?"

Patience is the habit or fact of being patient. Patience is also bearing trials or pain without complaint, calmly tolerating a delay, waiting without edge or anger, tolerance, and acceptance of things you can't change. That's a whole lotta stuff to be in one word! To gain the quality of patience is to:

- Accept things you cannot change,
- Be prepared,
- Remain calm when others aren't,
- Realize mistakes & accidents happen, and
- Understand you must wait for some things.

If you are standing in line, and you have no option about standing in this line (you aren't able to come back later), and you have no control over either the people in front of you or the person or process at the other end, why get upset? Suggestions:

- Always carry a book, something to listen to, or something to occupy your attention in the event of delay.
- Allow time for delays in your schedule.
- Carry a healthy snack and water with you always.

- Talk to the people around you. This may help ease their frustration, and make you feel better too.

What if the patience you desire is at home, possibly regarding children. You may not be able to gain patience as easily as you gain (or lose) weight, but try these steps in your action plan. You may find they are just the extra umph you need to get things going in a positve direction.

1. Anaylze a typical 24-hour period in your week. When do you have the most and least patience?

2. Get a clear picture of what is going on (what activities are you and those around you involved in) during those times and write the activities with times and days of week in your Source Book.

3. Think of some ways to buffer the time when you have your least patience. As an example, let's say you work full-time and have two children over age 3 but under age 12, and they go to school and have some form of childcare.

A typical day may go like this. Wake up. Rush around the house getting everyone ready for school and work. Breakfast, homework, dressing, lunch preparation, hair, hygiene, and out the door at a set time. You drop the kids at school and commute more than 10 minutes to work.

At the end of the day you leave work, swing by and pick up the kids, and then pull into the grocery store to pick something up for dinner. The kids have their own needs and wants that may not coexist harmoniously with yours. After the grocery story drama, you arrive home on the verge of "something.'"

Chaos ensues. You have a glass of wine to unwind while making dinner. You shout at the kids to get their homework done before they can watch T.V. Throughout the evening you are being drained of energy until they're tucked into bed. You are so exhausted you collapse with another glass of wine.

Is any of this sounding familiar?

Are you going through some of the same things? Trying to find a balance between what you want done and what can reasonably be expected to get done can be difficult. Determine what is important to you—that you want accomplished during the schoolweek—and what can be completed when the demands of work and school no longer infringe on family time. Personally, I think having a little less stress and a little more clutter is okay. I find when I'm trying to keep the house clean, everything picked up, the laundry done, the dishes put away, and everything else... that I am stressed and uptight. Nowadays, my house isn't showroom clean and I no longer do the housework alone. These days, all are involved in the housework – but with less stess.

You might want to try a schedule or responsibility chart something like this:

Celia's Responsibility Chart (6 years old)		
Action	**Time**	**M T W TH F**
Lay clothes out for tomorrow	Before bed	
Put homework & needed items in backpack, put by front door	Before bed	
Bathe	Before bed	
Make bed	Before school	
Feed dog	Before school	
Wash face & brush teeth	Before school	
Complete homework	6-6:30 pm	
Nightly reading	Before bed	
Add any family meetings		

Adam's Responsibility Chart (9 years old)		
Action	**Time**	**M T W TH F**
Lay clothes out for tomorrow	Before bed	
Put homework & needed items in backpack, put by front door	Before bed	
Make bed	Before School	
Take out trash	Before School	
Wash face & brush teeth	Before bed/school	
Complete homework	6-6:30 pm	
Empty dishwasher	After school	
Nightly reading	Before bed	
Add any pet duties		
Add any family meetings		
Mom's Responsibility Chart		
Action	Time	M T W TH F
Lay clothes and accessories out for tomorrow	Before bed	
Put purse, briefcase by door	Before bed	
Make bed	Before work	
Pack lunches, prep items and leave in fridge	Night before, A.M. finish	
Play with kids, laugh, joke, talk for 10-30 minutes	15 min after arriving home	
Make dinner (with the kids help when feasible)	5:30pm-ish	
Help with homework	6-6:45 pm	
Nightly reading with kids	Before they go to bed	

2:12 Tips for Parents

Remember these important things when interacting with children:

- If you are stressed and angry, try to calm down before interacting with them. But do it without the alcohol (it becomes a crutch and you become dependent). Children often absorb our moods and we often do things, or say things, (when stressed) we wouldn't normally do or say.

- It's okay to tell them you are wrong or that you don't know the answer.
- A few minutes of one-on-one attention is so important. Try to carve out time to give each child individual attention, preferrably encompassing the childs' interests.
- It is important for you to have a couple minutes of alone time too.

Set yourself up for success and limit patience-draining activities when you are at your weakest. Avoid stressful situations, such as:

- Stopping at the grocery store after work with kids in tow (go there before picking up the kids);
- Rushed, disorganized morning routines (try making schedules);
- Homework time when you feel edgy and/or angry (reschedule it till later);
- Doing things when you're tired and hungry (that can be done another time), or doing them during important times in the child's schedule—thus disrupting it;
- Realize every child (including twins) is different.

That's an example of identifying issues and setting up an action plan. You can self-monitor for success, ask others if you are making improvement (more than likely they'll let you know if you are without asking), and add other ideas as well.

One of the most important steps in healing and/or growth that you can take is identifying the problem and the source of the problem. Often, we look at something we considered unrelated or minimally superficial we cast it aside as unimportant to "the scheme of things." Doing that, we often overlook critical aspects of our issue and never get to the root of the problem. Without the root, we can't weed out the problem or coax a solution to bloom. It (the problem) continues to reappear.

Open your Source Book and complete any exercises for Chapter 2, that haven' been completed. An action plan is included for your use.

While making changes to your thought process or habits, you may find yourself getting over-whelmed. This visualization exercise may help relieve some of the "mind" pressure. Place the CD in your player and participate in the "Changing Room" exercise.

2:13 The Changing Room Exercise

You can do this exercise anytime.

The following exercise is one I developed to relieve some of the pressures of everyday issues, negativity, or feelings of overwhelm.

(Insert disk into CD player and put on dream mask if you have one.) If a CD is not available, you can read through this paragraph once or twice, close your eyes, and then repeat the process in your mind. Or have someone you trust read the instructions to you.

You will remain seated at all times. During the exercise, you will mentally get up, and mentally walk. After the exercise is complete, you may wish to do a standing stretch, which is recommended.

To prepare, sit in a chair or on a couch just enough that your bottom is on the seat, but close enough to the edge that your hands should be able to dangle freely when not in your lap. Place both feet flat on the ground close together. Place your hands in your lap comfortably. Are you ready?

Close your eyes. Imagine you are in a room that is not too big, not too small, not too dark, and not too light. This room is perfect for you.

As you stand in the middle of the room, you reach out to the left side with your left hand. You reach until you touch the wall. Your hand travels along the wall, carefully feeling around. Your hand comes cross the nail hanging on the wall. The nail will not hurt you. It is not sharp or rusty or dangerous. Bring your left hand back to your side.

With your right hand you un-wrap the scarf that is unbearably snug around your neck. As the tails are unwound, you can feel the tension ease out of your neck. With both hands you hang your scarf on the nail and drop your arms to your side. Roll your head gently and slowly in a circular motion to remove any traces of tension or ache.

With your right hand you reach out in front of you and find the 2nd nail on the wall. This nail is there for you, it is not sharp or rusty or dangerous. With both hands, you tug that tight-fitting hat off your head. As soon as it is released, a slight breeze ruffles your hair. You hang the hat on the wall. Anxiety escapes as you run your fingers through your hair.

Again, with your right hand you reach out to the wall and move your fingers along the wall, through the corner seam, until you reach the wall on your right. You've come across the 3rd nail. This nail is there for you. It is not sharp or rusty or dangerous. With both hands you unbutton the heavy, suffocating jacket that has engulfed you. With each button unhooked, you release the pressure until you are able to shrug your shoulders and arms out of that jacket. You hang the jacket on the nail and slowly roll your shoulders backwards in a slow, controlled circle, allowing the built up tension in your back and shoulders to float away. As your muscles relax you feel as if you're weightless.

Rotate your shoulders slowly one more time. Now, place your right hand on top of your right shoulder and your left hand on top of your left shoulder. Keeping your hands on your shoulders, slowly rotate your arms—elbows pointing out—backwards in a circle and then backwards one more time. Let your hands come down and dangle along side your legs. Shake your fingers lightly, and imagine the stress releasing through those fingertips and splashing invisibly on to the floor. Gently shake those fingers. Roll your head slowly in one more full circle right, and then one slow circle left.

While still in a seated position, slowly bring your arms up over your head, lightly clasping your left hand around your right wrist. Extend your arms up gently. In a slow sweeping motion, release your arms back down to your side, immediately bringing your arms back up over your head, this time catching your left wrist with your right hand. Extend your arms up gently. Release your arms back to your side.

You reach into your pocket and draw out a key. You put the key in the door handle that is in front of you and you turn the key. The door opens, and you step outside. It is not too light and not too dark. It is not too cold or not too hot. It is just right. Replacing the key in your pocket you reach above you with both hands and stretch gently. Taking a deep breath, you stretch and exhale, inhale, exhale, and slowly bring your arms down to your side.

Slowly, you open your eyes. You are ready to go on with your day, knowing you have the key to unlocking your tension right in your pocket.

3:
Motivation

Motivation. What is it really? Motivation is the cause of a person's action, their WHY. It is said we move in the direction of our currently dominant thought. What are you thinking? When you lay awake at night awaiting sleep, what goes through your mind? Is your dominate thought about debt, responsibility, or an upcoming challenge? If so, then change it. Make your dominate thought a positive goal or big dream. Positive preparation before sleep primes positive thinking and creativity.

Motivation is made up of so many little things, little qualities, like little chunks of wishes. Are you motivated? If so, write in your Source Book whatever your motivators are and what you are motivated in.

I bet that question took a second read, a minute to ponder and think. What am I motivated in or toward? It's a hard question that needs serious consideration. Yet, as soon as you answer the question about what you are motivated in or toward, you must ask yourself why?

Why are you motivated toward this particular thing or destination? What is your driving force?

If you aren't motivated toward something or some destination, then you have to ask yourself, why not? Does this illuminate how important motivation is to our overall foundation, our overall self-worth, or even the overall structure of our self-image? If we aren't motivated toward something are we stagnating?

Realistically, some type of motivation is at work throughout our day, although it may be minor, mundane, or even damaging. The alcoholic works through the day to get to the next drink. The smoker watches the clock until break time to get a drag off a cigarette. The student crawls out of bed to attend a class that she may or may not be prepared for, but one which she must attend to receive a grade.

Each of these actions has a motivator, something to be accomplished and a reason behind it. But consider this. How much more satisfying would it be to be thankful you have a job to go to, a school to attend, or the ability to take a break.

Ask yourself that question again.

What are you motivated toward? Is it your deepest desire or even a far-fetched dream? Is it a pay raise? A good grade? A warm embrace? These are all valid motivators.

We can have many motivators and many mini-goals and many separate little dreams that require different paths, different materials, and yes, different motivators.

Are you going from day to day without purpose?

Can you account for your day with a meaningful accomplishment somewhere within those 24 hours? If not, what do you need motivation in? What are some small steps you can you start with so the whole motivation thing isn't so big?

3:2 Motivation and Change

Sometimes, it's like getting back into exercise. Starting something is difficult, *especially when that something is motivation itself.* But you can do it. I know you can. Think about something you want to get motivated about. The typical ones are job, exercise, and eating healthy, but I am going to use *be a better parent or animal owner* as an example. If you're not a parent or an animal owner, then skew this example to reflect something you can identify with.

I want to become a better parent/animal owner (hereafter known as P/A). *This doesn't mean I lump children and animals as the same obligation or source of joy. But as a parent and an animal owner, there are enough similarities here for our purpose.*

First, I would first look at what I presently do as a P/A.

- Do I feed them healthy food at the proper times?
- Are they and their environment kept clean?
- Do they receive enough exercise?
- Am I involved in their education or training?
- When I speak, is my tone pleasant? Does it convey care, love, and respect?
- When they require corrective action or punishment is it fair, just, and timely? Is it non-abusive and non-damaging?
- Do I ensure they are protected against the elements?
- Do I ensure they receive regular check-ups and immunizations?
- Have I made a memory with them today?

After asking myself all the applicable questions above, then I would ask myself, "Do I know why I want to be a better P/A?"

If any of these answers are <u>no</u>, then I would want to be

51

motivated to change. What could I do? Some actions I could take (and have taken) to become a better P/A are listed here.

(MY EXAMPLE)

During the school year I make time every day to talk with my son about his day. I find out what he did in class, what his homework is, (review his homework), what his upcoming assignments are, talk about specific lessons, what he had for lunch, how his friends are, and so forth. Granted, these are usually Q-A-Q-A-Q-A and not too deep, but they are a springboard for more in-depth questions when I see the need.

We play a board game, card game, or dice game at least twice a week. We often watch a TV show together 2-3 times a week.

We exchange hugs, kisses, pats on the back, and I love you throughout the day.

We eat at least one meal together daily and almost always dinner.

He has chores and a small allowance so I nag him daily (mostly in a good way.)

Once in a while he'll get involved in meal preparation with me or dad and that is always fun.

When he was younger, I'd have lunch with him at his school a few times a month.

Nothing I wrote here is earth-shattering or new insight. There is nothing especially unusual in my efforts. But I'll tell you something; I've heard the average amount of time a parent spends talking with their child is **SEVEN** minutes a day cumulatively. I'm sure I can make more time in my schedule for my child than seven minutes!

If I allowed my son (I know because my girls did it) to

come home from school and go to his room, I wouldn't see him until he came to the kitchen to forage for food or he went out the front door to play. *It takes motivation and effort to have a relationship* with children, with pets, and with adults.

As the children get older, it's even more difficult to capture their attention and their time.

> *The relationship cultivated early*
> *remains fruitful longer, especially with tending.*

If you are reading this and feel like you've been punched in the chest because you don't have that relationship with your child, don't fret. It is never too late to start; it is just more difficult.

Picture the relationship as a garden. There are overgrown weeds (needs), surface roots (hurts not mended, bad habits), and bare spots (questions, curiosities, desires.) With attention, a beautiful garden can grow anywhere as long as the gardener has used materials native to the environment. Which means it's often best to start a relationship by discovering what is there, and what can be used as a foundation, not demanding change and new design at the start.

Use the space in your Source Book to write what you wish to become more motivated about.

3:3 Ways to Get Motivated

These are some of the ways I've found to motivate myself:

- Think of actions that make you feel good, about yourself, your life, and your surroundings or environment.

- Do something every day (or multiple times during the day) to make you feel motivated, invigorated, or happy.
- Let go of any choke-hold the past has on you. If you've had failure before, it doesn't mean you'll fail every time. If you've done a wrong that you can't right, apologize sincerely. If the person you've wronged is not able to receive your apology, pray for forgiveness. If someone has done you wrong, forgive them completely. Let them know you have forgiven them whole-heartedly, or know in your heart you have.
- Immediately **stop** *doing actions you know are wrong.* It is impossible to liberate motivation within when guilt is your cloak. Whether it is a wrong to your body (smoking, drugs), or a wrong to another person, find a way to stop.
- Heal your body and your spirit.
- Learn from your mistakes, remember your successes (even the small ones), and seek new goals or milestones.
- Dream and dream big. Be excited about your dreams and **write them down**. Writing down your dreams adds validity, and you can read them or recite them everyday.
- Appreciate your surroundings. Do you have yucky surroundings? Find something to appreciate.
- Care for those whose lives you touch. Tell or show them you care in positive, frequent ways.
- Smile.
- Laugh.
- Contact others you care about and that care about you. Keep in touch.
- Be a friend (but not a doormat or sponge.)
- Take a moment and stretch your limbs.
- Look for true role models. Many people have overcome challenges to succeed. Learn their stories. They'll have something to share with you, or warn you away from. Be careful though.
- A true role model doesn't walk on others to get ahead.

- Role models treat living things with respect, without violence and without hostility.
- Notice and celebrate the positive steps you've taken and changes you've made.
- Exercise.
- Use time wisely. You can never make it up once it's gone.
- Have a safe harbor (place) to go to when things are stressful or hectic. Know *it* will pass, but if you want *it* to be different, it takes the personal courage to change. Find something to love about yourself. Accept you for who you are-flaws and all.
- If you have a tried and true method of self-motivation, use it. It (motivation) is not like a paper towel. When it works, use it and re-use it.
- Use the exercise at the end of Chapter 2 to relieve stress.
- Add your motivating factors in your Source Book.

3:4 Keys to Motivation

Remember. A key to motivation is to:

- **Focus on your desire** (the desire must be yours.) Why? If you are doing something for say ... your husband (like losing weight), and he doesn't notice, then what? You're crushed. But if you are losing weight because you'll feel better, have more energy, and alleviate some possible health concerns, then you are on the right track. It is your desire to make yourself healthier. The happy husband is just an added bonus.
- **Focus on the success**, not the failure. Why? Let's look at the diet. You are focused on losing weight. You post pictures of skinny people, negative posters, such as "You're fat. Don't eat that nasty stuff!"

What happens? Your mind doesn't process "don't." For example, if I were to say, "Don't think of pink elephants."

What would you think of, why pink elephants, of course. Or, if you had a slice of cake in front of you, and someone said, "Don't eat that cake." What do you want? That cake.

- Another example of a way to look at things positively or in a different focus is to focus on the success of your improved eating habits. A diet means restriction and denial. Consider telling yourself you are learning to eat healthier and take better care of your body instead of saying, "I'm going on a diet."

As I was, when focusing on the success of your improved eating habits you'll focus on your clothes fitting better, the improved movement of your limbs, the breath you still have after climbing stairs. You'll find you are more positive in mind and more likely to continue with the improved habits. Habits = change. When you continually and repeatedly do something, you are making a lifestyle change. Let's do it for the good.

- **Focus on the "why"** to stay on purpose. Why? To make a lifestyle change, a thought process change, or an image change – the purpose, the reason – the WHY must stay in sight. Lose sight of the why – and you'll go off track. A perfect tool for remembering your "WHY" is a "My Options Reminder" or M.O.R.
- **Purposely say**: I want to … I can … I will …

Visualize: Doing what you want, doing what you can, doing what you will, and visualize achieving your goal.

Replace fear motivation with desire motivation. Get the complete details of what you want and what you strive for. It adds to the visualization process. Make *your* desire your dominant thought. What are your current desires?

Visualize what you want and write the details in your Source Book.

4:
The Ingredients of Self-Worth

To define self-worth, I suggest looking at each base word separately. The self is the total, essential, or particular being of a person, the qualities that separate them from another, or one's consciousness of one's own being or identity. You can't get much deeper than that.

Worth, for our purposes, is defined as equal in value to and deserving of, the value measured by its qualities, moral or personal merit, or the quality that renders something desirable, useful, or valuable. Everyone has value, some measurable worth.

We can say then self-worth is the essential qualities an individual possesses that make them unique, desirable, and valuable in their own way.

Although there are more than 100 self-(something) combinations, such as self-destructive, self-centered, self-assured, or self-reliant, I feel there are specific ingredients that are the basis of a positive self-worth. These ingredients make up the acronym DARCIE:

Deserving
Acceptance
Respect
Confidence
Integrity
Esteem

Ask yourself: If you don't nourish you, or feed your soul, or love you for who you are, then who will?

Now ask yourself these questions:

- WHO is the most important person in your life? (The only correct answer is YOU.)
- Why should you feel undeserving?
- What about you should you not accept?
- How can you respect others without first respecting yourself?
- Do you believe that you were born with confidence, or that confidence is learned?
- Is integrity easily attained or a daily virtue one must strive to hold on to?
- Is it conceited to hold "you'" in esteem?
- Is thankfulness of your talents wrong?
- Is tolerance only for others?
- Can trustfulness apply to your feelings too?
- Are you trustworthy?
- Does a caring, compassionate heart apply to you as well as those you care about?

All of these questions and their answers are critical to developing your self-worth. Some of them overlap in virtue and definition to the other foundational qualities we've discussed so far. This is to be expected. All nine qualities will overlap to some degree, because each one is important to your inner thoughts, beliefs, actions, and feelings.

Marianne Williamson wrote a phenomenal poem I can

relate to. You've probably heard of it. "Our Greatest Fear" was included in *Return to Love* (Harper Collins, 1992) and recited in the movie, "Coach Carter."

The poem is significant in the discovery process, in the acceptance process, and in the building process as a person grows inside. In the poem, she suggests when we play down our self or belittle our accomplishment(s); we are doing a disservice to those around us. (I've included a few lines):

> *...And as we let **our own light shine**,/we unconsciously give other people/permission to do the same. ...* (emphasis is mine)

The poem is so poignant that it brings tears to my eyes even now, even after I have read it several times.

I used to be afraid to "let my own light shine," in anything that I did. I owned a company but instead of reveling in my success, strength, and responsibility, subconsciously I pretended I was an employee, one of the managers instead of the owner. I'd say things like, "We do" or "We teach" instead of saying, "I."

I was self-defeating insomuch that I didn't stand up and say, "I did this, me." Everything was 'we' although there wasn't a mouse in my pocket or a partner or an employee.

Be the brilliant, gorgeous, talented, and fabulous" person you were made to be instead of "playing small." It's in there. Maybe it's deeply hidden, but everything you need to begin a life of loving your self first, of finding *and* accepting your self-worth, is inside of you.

Let's look at how we can address each of the self-worth ingredients, and discover methods we can use to strengthen those that need some help.

4:2 Self-worth Ingredient: Deserving

Deserving is the first ingredient of self-worth. When you are considered deserving, you are worthy of merit. You have a quality or virtue that has earned praise or approval. You have demonstrated ability or achievement and superior worth.

If you lay on the couch all day for no other reason than laziness or boredom, what are you deserving of? Boredom, muscle failure, back problems ...etc.

If you are unemployed, yet attending developmental schools, seeking employment, and otherwise trying to better yourself, what are you deserving of? I'd say you are deserving of attaining your goal.

4:3 Self-Worth Ingredient: Accepting

Accepting is the second ingredient in a positive self-worth. It sounds so simple. Accept who you are right now. That is a simple sentence, true, but a difficult endeavor. What is acceptance? It is seeing something as satisfactory. It is saying something has worth, that it is able to satisfy a need, requirement, or standard, that it is usual or right, and that it is regarded as true or believed in. Any of those statements and any of those specific actions or beliefs are accepting and acceptance.

Do you find it difficult to accept who you are? I realize you have some characteristics or qualities you'd like to change or you wouldn't be reading this book. But before you can grasp the *'new you'* it is important to come to terms (acceptance) with the *'old'* you.

Think for a moment of the specific thing or things you don't like about yourself. Jot them down in your Source Book.

Are they severe deformities or minor issues? Are they embarrassing to you, or just something you wish wasn't there? Are they something you can change?

Regardless of what you don't like about yourself, and realizing the actual process of accepting your 'flaws' may be a tad difficult, realize it is possible.

Once you learn to accept yourself, you are on the way to positive self-worth. Try these immediate corrections to your thoughts:

If your usual thought is:	Think or do this instead:
I'm not smart enough to do this!	*I am prepared. I will do my best.*
I'm such a klutz!	*I won't rush around or carry so much that I can't see where I'm going.*
I look like crap!	*I'll take the time & effort with my appearance so I'll look my best.*
They won't like my idea!	*I'll keep my emotions detached; they are looking at my idea, not me.*

Write other thoughts or actions I can learn to accept about ME in MY Source Book.

4:4 Self-Worth Ingredient: Responsibility

Responsibility, the third ingredient in self-worth, is nothing short of essential. Can you be irresponsible for yourself—irresponsible to yourself—and still show responsibility for others? I think not.

To me, accepting responsibility for one's self and acting responsibly is a precursor to accepting responsibility for others. What does self-responsibility entail? Responsibility is taking care of your health and your body, demonstrating concern and commitment with your choices, and being accountable for your thoughts and actions.

An example of irresponsibility is demonstrated by an alcoholic. Although alcoholism is a disease and requires treatment to effectively control the symptoms, it is the irresponsible person that goes without treatment.

My mom was an alcoholic, and her alcoholism played a significant part—it may have been the key reason—of some of my more difficult adolescent years.

Once she became inebriated, she became undependable. I never knew what she would say or how she would act. It's been more than 30 years, and I can still remember, vividly, some of her actions and words. After a few drinks, all of the hurt and anger and frustration and dissatisfaction she normally kept inside would gush out like a raging river bent on destructing what was in her path (usually me).

I call this irresponsible. Her lack of responsibility to herself, her health, and the emotional well being of her children resulted in serious health issues for herself, and emotional issues for her children. How could she, or you, or I become more responsible to our self?

Start by being honest. Have you let yourself go, putting healthy habits off till tomorrow instead of doing today?

Have you allowed a 'crutch' to get you through the day, the job, or the issue? Has your crutch become a dependency and interfered with a positive, healthy lifestyle? Has your crutch caused you to become irresponsible with others?

Do you have an excuse for everything that goes awry?

Get help. If you have an unhealthy habit or dependency, please get help. It is not a weakness to admit you have a problem or a disease. The weakness comes from thinking you can do everything yourself. At the back of the book are a few websites and hotline numbers for some of the more common life/dependency issues.

Be realistic. If you have had some failures in the area of responsibility, watch for what you sign up for or agree to. Remember the assessment in the front of the book? Saying 'yes' to too many things or assuming responsibility for too much (in addition to the responsibility you already have) can overwhelm you, and then you may feel the stress of performing, or, if you don't come through, the miserable feeling of failing.

Be accountable. If you have taken on a responsibility you are unable to complete or uphold, then contact the person you received the responsibility from as soon as you realize you aren't able. In the case of parenting, if you are feeling overwhelmed there are support groups and services that can help you. But first you must be accountable for your feelings and your limits.

Learn from mistakes. Everybody makes mistakes. It is important to be able to take away lessons learned and for you not to repeat those mistakes. When you make a mistake, think about what went wrong and how you could do it right. If possible, correct the wrong.

Change unhealthy habits to healthy ones. I like to eat junk food as much (or maybe more) as the next person. But I also know how it affects my body and destroys my weight-loss and weight-maintenance goals. I believe in moderation instead of abstinence.

I *used* to smoke, but I quit that (thankfully) well over 9 years ago. I drink occasionally, but *refrain* from getting drunk. I *have become* responsible and don't drive within two hours after consuming one drink. I exercise, but not on a strict regular routine. *I have habits I need to change as well.* I subscribe to an ongoing reflection. How am I doing? What am I doing right? What needs improvement? *I believe it is my responsibility to look at my habits regularly, because they change as my environment and time constraints change.*

What are some other ideas you have for becoming more responsible? Yes, write them in your Source Book.

4:5 Self-Worth Ingredient: Confidence

Confidence is the fourth ingredient to a positive self-worth. How many times have you heard, "You just have to have confidence in yourself?" More times than you can count on both hands and both feet I'm sure. Yet, it is difficult to learn to have confidence in yourself if you weren't taught the steps. Yes, even self-confidence (a learned thought and a learned behavior) has steps to building.

Often, you see a parent allowing their child to sit up on their own, pull themselves up, take their first step. Each of these actions builds confidence. A baby doesn't wake up one morning and decide to walk. It is a process from holding the head up, sitting up, pulling up, standing, holding on to something and taking a tentative step and, eventually, walking without support. Even in generalization that is seven steps.

I feel confidence can be divided into six parts that make up the whole. They're my "Keys to Confidence," and they are:

1 – Find a true interest   2 – Become knowledgeable
3 – Lose the prejudices   4 – Communicate assertively
5 – Posture and projection
6 – Become comfortable with the body

4:6 Keys to Confidence

Key #1 – Find a TRUE Interest

An easy method to mess up someone's head is to make them feel uninteresting. "Nobody cares what you think." "You don't know what you're talking about." "You are so boring!" Comments like these erode someone's confidence.

When you have an interest, one that is yours alone, (doesn't require someone else to participate), you may discover it is an excellent way to build confidence because it is something you can either take pride in, become good at, or use your interest as a building block for something else. Because it's an interest you have, there isn't the hesitation often associated with trying something new because you release the need to "know how to do it" immediately, and give yourself the permission to *learn h*ow to do it. "An interest" allows time to explore and see if it is something you like, something you may want to spend time doing, or you may find it isn't for you at all.

How do you find and interest and where do you look? Here are some ideas to get you started:

Art	Individual or group sport
Collecting	Designing objects
Designing Interiors	Crafts
The Stock Market	Models (build/paint)
Music	History
Computers	Electronics
Wild Life Study	Graphics
Finance	Oceanography
Meteorology	Investments
Government	Conservation
Jewelry	Writing

A true interest has your passion. You are compelled to learn, know, and be your passion. For every imaginable interest there is a magazine or how-to book. The library is a great place to begin your research. If none of the topics on the list jumps out at you, do a little research. Maybe something you were passionate about or find even remotely interesting develops into something else. That's okay. You are growing.

When you are developing an interest, *especially as you are building your confidence in yourself*, you'll want an interest that is *exclusively* yours. Look for something you can do with alone, without your friend, boyfriend, or husband. When you try and tie your interest in with someone, problems arise. Competition. Jealousy. Loss of interest. If this interest is just for you, you can excel and feel good about yourself.

Why do I think it is important to have a true interest? Besides giving you something to do, being interested in something and devoting time to it usually results in being competent in it.

Let's say you were interested in basketball. You would learn how to play the game, the rules, how to hold the ball, do tricks, make baskets, and so forth. If you were really interested in it (passionate about it) you would, in time, become good at it. Being good at something is a confidence builder.

Let's look at another topic, one that isn't so easy. Say you enjoy fine art. You don't have to be in a position to *own* something for it to hold your interest, or for you to be good at it. You study it, you learn it, you know everything there is to know about your style or period of art; who, what, where, when and how much it is worth.

Your passion for fine art can lead you to a fulfilling career dealing with art as an appraiser, a buyer, or a museum curator. Or it can remain something you enjoy, and something you are good at.

Your confidence is raised by the knowledge or possession of a talent. So Key #1 recommends finding an interest that is true to you and your personality.

Key #2 – Become Knowledgeable

Whatever your age, dumb isn't cute, and dumb isn't sexy. Confidence and power require smarts. The kind of smart I'm talking about doesn't include a degree or PhD. It does require you learning about your surroundings and basic education though. Sexiness and cuteness come from confidence, from knowledge. You can become knowledgeable if you

- Take some classes to learn something new;
- Know what's going on in the world;
- Be involved in your community;
- Continually seek new knowledge.

Learn basic math skills, reading skills, and writing skills. The more you learn and on a broader scale, the more confidence you will have carrying on a conversation or stating an opinion. The ability to carry on an intelligent conversation and state an opinion with the knowledge and confidence to support that view is exciting and interesting, and it opens doors and invites further dialogue. Can you honestly say you wish people found you less interesting, and more boring?

If politics, social occurrences, community events, or anything is unclear to you, talk to people about them. Read about them. If it doesn't sound right or it doesn't make sense, investigate. Becoming knowledgeable is fascinating. It expands your horizons, your contacts, and yes, other interests too, because you learn of new things you didn't have a foundation of knowledge for.

Are you afraid to show your smarts because someone may expect more of the same? Fear of something isn't respect. Respect is appreciating the knowledge, skill, or integrity of another. Those qualities (and opinions) can be different then yours, but you can respect them just them same. Expect you will have knowledge, skills, and opinions different than others. Expect not everyone will agree with you. This is normal. Just because someone doesn't share your viewpoint doesn't mean you should pretend to be dumb or ignorant.

Smart *is* sexy. Knowledge *is* sexy.

Becoming knowledgeable can encourage compassion, and if not acceptance of the difference in others, at least a better understanding. See how knowledge is a key for you?

Key #3 – Lose the Prejudices

Skin color *does not define* you unless you allow it to or unless you conduct yourself in a negative stereotypical manner. Someone else's skin color *does not define* them unless they conduct themselves in a negative stereotypical manner. *Actions speak louder than skin color.*

As you grew up, your environment shaped and molded you. Maybe your parents are first generation immigrants or maybe they're in this country illegally. Maybe your parents' parents were slaves or maybe slave owners, people abusers, confederates, British army or whatever.

With today's diversity mix, melt, and topping we are, together, one big ice cream shake, salad, or melting pot, however you want to look at it. Very few people are purebred any things. How can you be prejudice?

You, as an individual, should consider that your parents have bestowed their beliefs upon you either directly (verbal) or indirectly (actions). It is up to you to adopt your own beliefs and recognize there are differences in cultures. Celebrate it. Learn about it.

Confidence in self is built by understanding differences in others. Notice I said understanding. I did not say liking or approving, but understanding the differences and accepting *that there are* differences.

What shaped the beliefs your parents and grandparents have could have been terrible, humiliating, degrading or racist. Or it could have been wonderful, supportive, uplifting, and diversified. If you feel bias or prejudice were present while you were growing up, or you feel those thoughts influence you, then maybe it's in your best interest to learn the history and form your own beliefs from the information you find.

Personally, I believe there isn't a lot of room in a caring and confident heart, mind, and body, for feelings of superiority.

The Key to Confidence #3—and building confidence in you—is losing the prejudice, learning about differences, and celebrating who *you* are, even if you are 1/3rd Black, 1/3rd Asian, and 1/3rd White. Just think of the cultural richness you CAN possess.

Key #4 – Communicate Assertively

Learn to communicate effectively. Do you have a problem, concern, or issue? Do you bottle it up inside? Do you replay it over and over again, allowing the anger or resentment to build?

If you learn to speak your mind, you develop confidence in yourself and know that your opinions matter. What you think does matter. Always believe it does.

Now, I am not, repeat NOT, saying its okay to cuss at your parents, children, family, or friends. Learning to communicate effectively allows you to state what is on your mind without raising the defenses of another, at least not excessively.

There may be some learning curves involved here and it will take effort. But the rewards are well worth the work. A mother/daughter example is:

Mother: "How was school today?"

Daughter: "Fine."

Mother: "What did you do/learn?"

Daughter: "Nothing."

Mother: "Nothing?"

Daughter: "I don't know. We learned some stuff." Then daughter retreats to her bedroom.

What has anyone gained from that conversation (or word exchange)? They gained nothing. Did it seem like the daughter cared that her mom was interested enough to ask? No. The daughter could have thought the mom was being nosy and it wasn't her business or that she wouldn't understand. Step parents and children find this word exchange even more invasive and upsetting.

Let's say the teen discussed above had a day that actually went like this:

She put makeup on while she was going to school. At school she pulled her over-shirt off to reveal the cute tee underneath. When she got to school, a group of girls slammed her up against her locker for a "joke," which put a gash on her shoulder from the rusty metal. Her hair pretty much covered the bloodstain.

In history, she got a "D" on a quiz, her 3rd one, which required detention. At lunch, her best friend wasn't talking to her because of what happened last night.

As the teen sat there drinking her diet drink and eating pepperoni pizza, the boy she has a crush on walked by. He happened to look at her right as she stuffed the pizza into her mouth, which oozed sauce down her chin.

If that weren't enough, another girl that liked the same boy came over and called her a slut. That only covered periods 1–4!

School was fine? Do you really think mom doesn't care? Wouldn't talking about some of these issues be good? Aren't there some health and safety concerns?

For Example: A tetanus shot might be needed, and schoolwork issues need to be addressed, such as identifying distractions, workload, study habits, learning challenges, and chores. Together they could make a plan to improve struggling courses, set study times, learn techniques, and find alternate methods for learning classroom material.

It would be healthy to talk about her feelings related to being pushed into the locker, receiving detention, embarrassment about seeing the boy while eating, and getting called a slut.

Another scenario: Say you're late for work. When you arrive, you find out you have an important impromptu meeting you weren't prepared for. Then you realize you have two different shoes on. As you rush to prepare for the meeting, you spill coffee on your blouse (right down the front) that your jacket won't cover.

Your meeting goes okay, but then your mate calls to cancel lunch. You end up eating alone at your desk, and the phone rings incessantly. Your drive home is a slow chug through immense heat and smog. You can feel your lungs blackening and clogging as your car crawls through traffic.

You arrive home later than usual and are expected to make dinner, bathe the children, and do laundry. Your mate says, "So, how was your day?"

Do you keep it all bottled up inside? Do you explode like a volcano? Or do you take a deep breath and start with what was good about the day and weave the imperfections in?

Getting your feelings out into the open strengthens your self-confidence. Why? Because being able to identify what you feel is a gigantic part of self-worth and self-confidence. Identifying your feelings allows you to work through them and put them behind you. What were some of the feelings described above? Frustration? Embarrassment? Irritation? Those are just a few feelings the person in the scenario above would probably be feeling.

Why keep all that inside? Except causing ulcers, migraines, hormone imbalances, and a host of other problems, there is not a reason to keep all those feelings bottled up.

Did you tell what your feelings are? Were you able to communicate without biting the other person's head off? Give validity to your feelings, and allow the anger or frustration you feel to dissipate and go away by tactfully sharing the dilemmas of your day.

Effectively communicating is good for your body and good for your self-confidence.

What if, though, you're in a situation where stating your opinion isn't acceptable or possible? Or you have a mate that is self-absorbed in their own issues and isn't interested in what is going on with you?

Many of today's adults come from an era of "children should be seen and not heard" or "when I want your opinion, I'll give it to you", or even the cruel one, "what you think doesn't matter."

Repeat after me: "I pity the narrow-minded, developmentally challenged person that was so misled, and I forgive you, but I will not accept your belief nor impose that belief on my future children. I promise."

For any of you that have that obstacle (the narrow-mindedness), and it is an obstacle, you will have to work extra hard to change those thoughts and beliefs. So many people were raised without a voice and then ridiculed, because, as adults, they were unable to effectively state their opinion or thought because they weren't accustomed to voicing one.

A key to confidence is the belief what you *say* matters. Additionally, with confidence you believe what you *think* matters. If you never say anything or think anything, how can you boost your self-confidence? That goes back to Key #2

Key #2 says become knowledgeable. Learn basics, learn broader. State your <u>informed</u> opinion in class or at work. You can be confident because you'll KNOW why you think this way because you'll have researched it. If there is disagreement, you'll be able to debate it without hysterics because it's not only your opinion you feel this way but because "A, B, C" support your opinion.

If there is still disagreement, you can use Marla Stone's method: (example) I feel dismayed you don't agree with my position, and I respect the importance of differences in opinion. Then leave it alone and don't take it as an affront against you personally.

You have confidently stated your opinion and gotten those feelings off your chest. You no longer have to carry them like baggage.

Key #5 – Posture and Projection

Do you walk hunched over, head down, eyes down, stand with shoulders bowed with your arms across your chest?

Do you sit in the back of the room or away from the main people in the meeting?

When you stand someplace, do you cross your arms over your chest, stand hunched over, or stand with legs shoulder width apart with a mean look on your face?

73

Confidence is exuded when you walk with your head high and your eyes alert. Wear a smile on your face, and smile at others. Here are some tips to carrying yourself well.

- Stand or sit straight. Never, ever hunch.
- Wear the right clothing for the situation. Make sure your clothing is clean, pressed, and fits correctly.
- Be clean. Practice good personal hygiene.
- Know where you are going and how to get there.
- Be aware of your surroundings.
- Walk with a purpose.
- Discard the gum from your mouth before talking.
- Don't point at people.
- Maintain your own space without invading others'.
- Be interested in others. Listen to what they have to say.
- Try to maintain control of your emotions when angry or irritated (difficult, but possible with practice.) Try not to raise your voice, cuss, or show violence.
- Speak clearly. Make sure the other person understands what you are saying.
- When wearing perfume or body spray, make it a hint, just a tease that is barely there.

Visualize people you have seen walking lately. Did they walk with their head bowed as if they were making sure they didn't walk on a crack? Were their shoulders hunched over? Did they look like they were trying to fold into themselves?

Can you picture them? If so, what was your opinion of them? Did you think they were strong, capable people that you could like and trust? Or did you think them insecure, nervous, and afraid?

When you are walking someplace, anyplace, remember to walk with your head up, eyes alert and looking straight ahead. From time to time, look to your left and then to your right to see what is happening. Notice I said from time to time and not often. If you are looking around often, you look nervous and afraid.

Carrying yourself well is an easy way to "fake it 'till you make it." You can look like a confident, self-assured person immediately, even while you're learning to feel better about yourself and build your confidence.

Key #6 – Be Comfortable with Your Body

How can you be comfortable with your body when there are things you are not happy with, and there are things you want to change?

The first thing to realize is that there are things you can change and things you can't. So for that I have some ideas about what you may be thinking, (just some common issues we girls have) and if none of these are your issue, good for you. You will be able to look at them, laugh, and hopefully feel for those of us that have them.

Image Indicators

When you think about yourself, what do you envision? Are you attractive or plain, pretty or ugly? Are you heavyset, well-proportioned, skinny or fat? Can you walk with poise, or do you slump? Can you speak with confidence, or are you self-conscious and think no one wants to hear what you say. When you do talk, is it in an audible voice, or is it so soft people have trouble hearing you?

Image indicators, as I call them, are the thoughts and feelings you have in regards to your body. If, in your mind, you want to be a petite blonde with legs up to your shoulders, and you are actually five foot nine with short legs, an apple shape and red hair, you are going to have some issues about what you look like. This results in a negative personal image. Image, as I see it, relates to everything external about our body and some internal qualities as well.

Height: Although we can't exactly change our height, there are ways to look taller or shorter, depending upon the need. To become taller, heels are the obvious first choice, but not always practical. **To be taller:** You can appear taller by wearing a long, flowing skirt that reaches the ground. Pants should be floor length and either wide at the bottom or straight legged with at least a 2-inch heel. **You'll appear shorter** when wearing something that has patterns across or around. This breaks up the line. Ankle length/cuffed pants make legs appear shorter. Flat shoes make legs appear shorter.

Weight: A hard, hard subject to discuss. I think I have only met one person in my life (really, *my life*) that was happy with the way she was RIGHT NOW. Whatever size, whatever shape, she was happy. Good for her.

For the rest of us, weight can be a healthy motivator or a self-esteem nightmare. Realize that it is your choice—yes!—your choice on which route to take.

If you think you are too skinny, eat healthy, watch your good fat/bad fat intake, and exercise regularly. You may, with the help of a doctor or certified trainer, begin a weight-training regime to tone and strengthen your muscles.

There are many muscles you can enlarge to gain the appearance of bulk. Choose clothing that is not skin-tight or too baggy, but not fitted either. Horizontal stripes make you appear wider, as do round collars just above your chest. Low-on-the-hip pants make your hips look wider when you wear a top that reaches your belt loop.

If you think you are too heavy, then eat healthy, watch your good fat/bad fat intake, and exercise regularly. Refrain from fad diets or plans with severe restrictions and denials.

Get on a healthy program and allow rewards for achievements. Vary your menu and try new things. Consider, with the help of a doctor or certified trainer, beginning a cardio- and weight-training regime to tone and strengthen your muscles. Working with weights is an important part of weight loss. Not all weight training results in bulking up. More repetitions with lower weights help burn calories and tone your muscles. This promotes a sleek appearance.

An aerobic exercise regularly performed motivates the metabolism to burn calories. Before you start a weight-loss program, seek the advice of trained professionals, and do not—I repeat do not—starve yourself to lose weight.

Starvation may bring a temporary weight loss, but once you reach your desired weight and you resume eating, you'll pack the weight back on. What will follow is called yo-yo dieting. This is really bad for your system. Although it won't be a quick fix, eating healthy, reducing portions to an appropriate amount (this could be 1200–1800 calories), exercising 3–5 times a week (at least 3 days of cardio), and removing soda, chips, candy, sugars, sweets, and other non-healthy foods from your menu will jump start your weight loss.

Strong Features: How you view your strong features (if you have them) depends a lot on how you were treated when you were young. A beautiful, prominent nose can add character, an angled chin signifies strength. You have two choices when it comes to strong features: learn to love them and accentuate them, or have them altered.

The second choice is not recommended. Often, when you have a feature altered because of dissatisfaction with it, you are still unhappy with the results after the change has been made. It is a lack of self-confidence and self-esteem that keeps you from accepting the feature in the first place.

Changing it will not necessarily make you feel better about yourself. If you can come to accept and feel good about yourself even with the strong feature, you are miles (and dollars) ahead of those lacking in self-confidence and self-esteem.

Methods to learn acceptance are makeup techniques (for faces and scars), research, finding someone you respect that has the same or similar strong feature and hair style or selection.

Hair: Hair is one of the easiest characteristics to change about our self and often a fun one. What's important here is that we get a cut, style, and color that reflect our personality and lifestyle.

There are treatments available to change thin hair to wavy hair, and wavy hair to straight hair. Of course, there are also fabulous wigs when we want a temporary change.

Makeup: Soft, subtle shades are almost always the most flattering. Foundation that is oil-free is usually best on any skin.

Choosing the right makeup has never been easier with all the choices, but all those choices also make it more difficult. My book *Beauty Secrets You Can Use at Home* provides all the information and application techniques to help you look your best and choose the right color for all your makeup needs, choose the style that compliments your facial features the best, and also shows the application techniques.

As you can see, for every concern, there is a way to either alleviate the concern or find ways to accept what we have and turn a negative into a positive. A positive self image is an important part of a strong sense of self-confidence and self-worth.   Can you think of any additional keys to confidence? Write them in your Source Book.

78

4:7 Self-Image Questions

Now it's your turn to discover what you *really* think. In your Source Book, write down the first thing that comes to mind when you read the question. Don't think about it, just write. You'll be able to think about it later.

Ready? Remember, no deep thinking and no erasing.

1. You spent a long time getting ready to go out because you wanted to look your best. A friend said, "Wow. You look so good in that dress. You look amazing!" What would you say?

2. You and some friends were at the bowling alley having a great time. In between turns everyone munched on nachos and fries. As you brought the fry to your lips, someone you liked walked by staring at you. What crosses your mind and what do you do?

3. Right after that special someone walked by at the bowling alley, you saw one of your least favorite people wearing the cutest outfit, and looking like they just stepped out of the fashion magazine. Even their hair was perfectly in place. You touch your hair with your newly broken finger nails and think:

After you've answered the questions honestly, go back and read the questions and your answers again. Don't change anything.

Now, read some possible answers and see how you relate:

1. You spent a long time getting ready to go out because you wanted to look your best. A friend said, "Wow. You look so good in that dress. You look amazing!" What would you say? **Thank you.**

2. You and some friends were at the bowling alley having a great time. In between everyone munched on nachos and fries. As you brought the fry to your lips, someone you liked

walked by staring at you. What crosses your mind and what do you do? **You smile really big, say hi, and plop the fry in your mouth. Everyone has to eat.**

3. Right after that special someone walked by at the bowling alley, you saw one of your least favorite people wearing the cutest outfit, looking like they just stepped out of the fashion magazine, with their hair perfectly in place. You touch your hair with your newly broken finger nails and think: **What in the world is she wearing, doesn't she realize she is at the bowling ally? At least, I'm dressed right.**

If you didn't answer the questions in the same way or some other type of POSITIVE way, go back at look at the questions again.

For question #1: After someone recognizes that you made the effort to look nice, what else could you say but "Thank you." You certainly wouldn't want to say something like, "Yeah right. You're just saying that." You did go to the effort to look good, right?

For question #2: Most everyone eats fries, and we all KNOW they aren't good for you. Okay, so what. When you're out with friends having a good time, a little junk food isn't going to hurt you (too much). Even if you're on "calorie reduction" and not as light in weight as you'd like, you still need bonuses and treats. Otherwise, the denial of things you like will over-run the desire of what you're trying to accomplish. So your special someone saw you eating something. Big deal. They eat too.

For question #3: This is a no-brainer. Have you ever gone someplace and been dressed wrong? Did you feel uncomfortable? Did you think everyone was staring at you because you didn't have the right type of clothes on? Not this time, right? You and your stylish self are dressed (I hope) for fun and bowling. If you can have fun and look good, you're there. And please, bowling is always good for at least one broken nail.

The key to this exercise and to this section is: being positive about "you" is a must. If you answered questions 1, 2, or 3 with a negative answer, then you know you have some issues to deal with. If you answered negatively, what did it do for you? Did calling yourself a bad name or calling someone else a name make you feel better about yourself? I doubt it. Do you think it would have been more fun to realize you are fun, amazing, hungry, worthwhile, stylish, and sometimes break nails and have bad hair days? If you aren't positive about you, who will be?

The six "Keys to Confidence" are six easy ways to make you feel better about yourself. Reprogram, change the tune, re-invent. However or whatever terminology you want to put on it. No one can make you feel good about yourself (for a long-term and permanent time) if you don't already have it in you. And when you give people the power to shake or shape your confidence with their words, than you are giving up a whole lot of power!

If you are confident in yourself, your feelings won't be hurt because someone didn't think or say you look good, or that you are pretty, or smart, or funny, or anything. You carry that knowledge with you, and you don't have to look to someone else for approval. Yet when you receive those kind words, accept them for the truth they are with a sincere "thank you." You *are* beautiful.

On the previous pages, we talked about ways to accept things you can not change or things that are difficult and/or expensive to change.

Now we will talk about your "perceived" image. I bet, if you asked your closest friends what they thought were your best features and your worst, their opinion would differ from what you thought.

If you asked them what your best characteristics were, they would probably be different too.

Our perceived image—what we think others see—is often different than what they do see.

Here's an example. When I think about my age, I think I am a lot younger than I am. I feel young, pretty, and in shape. Yet when I see myself in a mirror, especially in bad light, I see the age in my face, the acne scars, the large thighs, and I immediately feel older and frumpy. My perceived image is changed to a new, negative perceived image, and I think others must be seeing this older, heavier person as well. Fear not, I *now have a handle on the whole frumpy perceived image -- so it's temporary.*

I may know my actual age, but people who meet me or talk with me on the phone **feel and hear** my energy. They are surprised when they learn my true age. You may be asking why they would find out this information. Well, as a skin care representative, sometimes my age comes up in the course of the conversation. I can hear the surprise in their voice when my age is discussed, so my perceived image is given a boost. I can continue to feel energetic and this positive energy keeps me going. It's this type of energy that helps me do things that are good for me, and helps me do things that make me feel even better about myself, like, exercise, eat right, and read positive, reinforcing things, like this book.

4:8 How Positivity Helps Your Image

When you are doing positive, reinforcing actions you tend to respect your self and your time more. You become more considerate too. Being a positive person attracts other positive people. Here are some ways to show your self-respect and consideration:

- Only do things you know are right. If it feels wrong or makes you uncomfortable, don't do it.
- Learn to say 'no.' Do only those things you want to do. This doesn't apply to homework, chores, or tasks required at your place of employment.
- Find the time to concentrate on you. Do things that are just for you and your enjoyment. Relish them.
- If you are earning money, make sure that you have a plan for what you are earning and save 10% of money you earn (each payday). You are never too young (or too old) to start saving, but the younger the better.
- Take time to dream.
- Perform positive self-talks every day when you wake up and every night before you go to bed.
- Make good use of your time. Time lost can never be regained. Time used well can be very memorable and/or rewarding.

Can you think of some additional methods to reinforce positive self-image or actions to demonstrate the positive outlook you have? Write your ideas in your Source Book.

4:9 Self-Worth Ingredient: Integrity

Integrity is the next ingredient in the mixture of self-worth. This binder is the steadfast adherence to an ethical code. It holds your worth together with honesty. Integrity makes you whole when you have the other ingredients present.

What I love about integrity is the soundness of action. When someone I am in contact with has integrity, I can believe them. I don't have to wonder if they are being honest or if they have another agenda. It is a wonderful feeling.

When I look at my integrity, I look at it as doing the right thing even when no one is watching. I try to keep that in mind in everything I do. Because it is my integrity and my actions that cause people to believe me or do business with me, I want my actions to match my words, words that are spoken or written.

If you have had a period of time in your life that you weren't demonstrating integrity, you may have a difficult time having people believe in you, respect you, or trust you. Once trust or respect is damaged or destroyed, it is difficult to get it back or repair it. Difficult, but usually not impossible.

What about integrity to yourself? If you have allowed others to dictate your thoughts, feelings, and actions, you'll have to learn to trust yourself. This is hard, especially when you haven't had success with it in the past.

To build your integrity or to earn others' trust requires the same steps. First, commit to honesty. In every facet that is possible, be honest. Note, if you are in a situation where confrontation is dangerous and honesty could cause you harm, consider getting outside help and intervention. Also consider taking it slow; allow the person suppressing you to see the change over time instead of in one fell swoop.

Next, determine what is acceptable and unacceptable. Integrity is standing up for what is right, so it's important to know where you stand.

Once you've committed to honesty and know what your values are, stick to them and do your best to live by them. If there are others in your life who don't agree or support your values and ideals, that goes back to the 2nd step. Remember, just because you've seen the light and are changing your ways (all in a week or a day,) don't expect people to believe it will last. Refrain from making ultimatums at the start.

Once you realize you can be honest, and once you've

decided what your values are, and after you successfully demonstrated actions consistent with your values, you'll find people (and yourself) will start taking this change seriously. It takes time for this to happen, and it takes consistency.

Soon, your integrity will bring self-respect and respect from others. It will build your feelings of self-worth tremendously.

What happens though, if you make a mistake or give in to temptation? Is all lost? Not necessary. Again, your actions will speak volumes. If you make a mistake, own up to it, be accountable, and accept responsibility for it. Do not, regardless of who else might have been involved, place blame on anyone else for your actions. You made your choice.

Clean up the mistake. Make amends. Apologize. Do whatever you can to make it right.

4:10 Self-Worth Ingredient: Esteem

The final ingredient in building self-worth is **esteem**. The definition of esteem is "to regard with respect." It also involves (1) consideration, (2) feeling of approval and liking, (3) friendly greeting, (4) pay attention to, (5) relate to, (6) have opinion of, and (7) look at.

An important step in building self-esteem is figuring out why it's low in the first place. Many people think it's normal and okay to call yourself (and others) names.

Often, people do it as a joke. They don't mean to hurt someone. This is seen a lot in brothers and sisters. Name calling, humiliation, teasing, and things like that. In most cases, it is done in jest, but for the one getting the wedgie, or the one who is being made fun of, it can hurt their feelings. Over time, they begin to believe the things they hear most. They think they are stupid and will call themselves that.

Another reason to learn what has caused the low self-esteem is to break the cycle. Let's say you are called lots of negative names. You hear it so often, maybe it's true. WRONG! If you allow yourself to believe this—a natural thing to do—it will make you expect to be treated like that all your life. You will think you deserve the low paying job, the horrible boss, the boyfriend that takes his aggression out on you.

Is there a name you were called that struck a bad note with you? Even if it was just once--it's like--*how dare you*! My father called me some horrible names during the period of time that I lived with him (about six months, over 20 years ago.) One word, which is so horrible I won't even write it here, has never left me. I cringe when I hear the word, even today.

I was driving home one day and started crying when I thought about it. In your Source Book, write the word, or words, you were called. Then write... No one should be called that. I am not a _____. I do not accept that label.

I'm here to tell you, you don't deserve to be degraded. You are worthy of a job you love with a good wage. You are worthy of being treated with respect, and you are no one's punching bag.

Do you agree? Or, are you your own worst enemy? Let's see. Answer these questions:

1. Do you communicate your basic needs?

2. Do you become silent when your needs are not met?

3. Do you allow yourself time to look at both sides of a problem before you react?

4. Do you spend quiet time with yourself to unwind, read, meditate, or pray?

5. Do you think about your day, both the happy and sad?

6. Do you seek understanding or mutual respect?

7. Do you find yourself doing the same routine every day?

It's easy to be our own worst enemy, especially when we have been primed since birth. Sometimes it's hard to communicate what we want, isn't it? But it is crucially important.

Our basic needs, from question #1, are referencing the needs Maslow describes in his hierarchy pyramid. The first four levels are:

1. Physiological: hunger, thirst, shelter, bodily comforts

2. Safety/security: to be comfortable in and with your surroundings, to be out of danger

3. Belongingness and love: be appreciated, be accepted, have a sense of commonness

4. Esteem: to achieve, be competent, gain approval, respect, and recognition

Look at some of the answers on the following page to see if they reflect your was of thinking, or, see if maybe you are setting yourself up for things (communication mishaps) unknown.

4:11 Communicating Needs

Comments to Question #1

Are you able to communicate your basic needs to the people in your life? What if your physiological needs are being met but you're afraid? Or what if you go through the day without a feeling of belonging, without feeling accepted?

Lacking any of those feelings or not fulfilling your basic needs will have serious consequences. I realize you may not be able to change your physical environment right now, and I realize change takes time. I also know to make the initial confession to your self that "all is not well" requires gumption, and acting on that realization takes courage.

It also requires communicating your needs to someone that can do something about it. Why be your own worst enemy? If you are (or feel) unsafe, tell someone. If your need for food and shelter is unmet, find a way to get it met.

When you put forth serious, consistent effort to make a better life, the forces of the universe will eventually come to your aid. It requires you to be proactive to make it happen.

Comments to Question #2

Oh my. I used to be the queen of passive aggressiveness. Fortunately, I have learned better communication methods.

Question 2 is about passive aggression. This method is about holding all the anger inside. After even a short period of time, and without a channel or an outlet, it feels like your insides are boiling and getting ready to burst. Suddenly you're slamming every cupboard door as you put away the dishes, speaking with mean a tone that could cut if it were a knife.

This is an unhealthy way to communicate your feelings. Amazingly, most of the time, the person you are fed up with doesn't get it, or they don't realize what has transpired, and you just get angrier. Do yourself a favor. Adopt a different communication style.

When you are angry, acknowledge the feeling and the process. Discuss without naming or blaming the other person. Chapter 7, communication, gives great guidelines for communicating effectively.

Comments to Question #3

If you're angry or feeling misunderstood, it is hard to look at both sides of a problem or an opinion. Dr. Covey states in his book, *The 7 Habits of Highly Effective People,* "If you seek first to understand, the other person will feel valued. She will be more open to listening to you if she feels you understand where she is coming from."

Do you feel valued when you are trying to get a point across and the person you're talking to stops what she is doing, looks at you, and listens to you all the way through ... without interrupting? That's giving and receiving value.

Questions four, five, and six are addressed elsewhere in the text, so I won't go into detail here, only to say that everyone needs alone time to collect their thoughts.

Comments to Question #7

Routines can be both good and bad. A good routine is something positive you do on a daily or regular basis. This could be a routine of waking up, saying your thanks, your affirmations, and then eating a healthy breakfast.

A bad routine is something you have allowed to happen. You come home from work or school, plop on the couch, eat chips, candy, and chocolate, guzzle a soda or have a drink, and watch the TV for hours. Nothing good will come from that. Get in the habit of doing good things every day.

4:12 Tips for Building Self-Worth

An important part of self-image and self-worth is how you react to what is going on around you. I don't know about you, but I've got to keep my self-worth intact and grounded. I have goals to achieve. I can't let other's dissatisfaction with life bring me down, or allow their doom and gloom to color my vision.

You probably know intrinsically not every one will cheer you on as you work to gain positive self-worth. You may have realized you will need to strengthen yourself for the barbs. To do this, you'll learn how to recognize your feelings without letting them overly influence or control you. This is also called detachment. With detachment, you can use both what you think and what you feel to make a decision.

It's important to realize not everyone wants you to succeed. It's also important to remember that many do. A definite, positive sense of self-worth is an important foundational quality to a happy, healthy, balanced you.

Build feelings of self-worth by using affirmations and these building techniques:

- Build your confidence. Use the "Keys to Confidence."
- Improve your perceived image. Compare yourself to your own goals.
- Show consideration and respect for yourself. Compare yourself to your own strengths.
- Remember: to yourself and to others, speak and act in a manner that actively encourages development in a positive way.
- Communicate your basic needs in a manner the listener can understand.
- Write your goals down and review them often.
- Daily, for about 20–30 minutes, dream and envision the acquisition of your dreams and desires. Do this for personal and professional development, as well as family enrichment. Ensure you know the specifics (color, size, and model) of your dreams.
- When someone gives you a compliment, say thank you.
- Refer back to the list where you wrote the qualities you admire about yourself. Write down some affirmations about your strong points, about the qualities you would like to improve. Remember to write them as if you currently possess those qualities. An example is:

I like myself.
I am worthy and provide worthwhile input.
I am beautiful inside and out.

- Practice talking good about yourself. Do it daily, at least five times throughout the day. Train your subconscious to think good thoughts. Supplement your words with pictures.
- Get rid of non-supportive, negative friends, or invite them to grow too.
- Journal your thoughts in daily, without editing.
- Dwell on rewards of success, instead of the penalties of failure.
- Respect yourself and others.
- Put only good thoughts or truth words into the universe.
- Be the type of friend you would want yourself.
- Have a portrait taken where you look exceptionally good. Look at it often.

In your Source Book, write additional ideas you have to strengthen your positive self-worth.

I believe I can be...
forgiving.
humble.
loving.
smart.
strong.
compassionate.

I can love others when I love myself.

I can make the difference in the world I seek to make, without losing myself.

If every cloud has a silver lining, then every action is an opportunity. Every opportunity provides choice. I choose to be optimistic. I choose to find the good in the bad. What is your choice?

5:
Optimism

Dr. Waitley says optimism is the single most outwardly identifiable quality of a positive self-image. I agree. Even if you consider yourself a confident person, if you possess skepticism or negativity, those undesirable qualities will hang like a black cloud around you.

Optimism is more than seeing the glass half full or half empty. Optimism is:

- Expecting favorable results from your actions.

- Looking at problems as opportunities.

- Praising instead of criticizing.

- Having an aura that's relaxed and friendly.

- Knowing you CAN make your dreams come true.

- Remembering faith conquers all.

If you have an attitude of inner faith, it'll generate an attitude of inner drive, motivation, and dedication.

When you put forth the effort, you should expect favorable results. Regardless of the task, do your best. Even if the environment is a hostile one, consistent demonstration of an excellent product, service, attitude, or state of mind is bound to crack the negative aura and allow goodness to seep in.

Problems and challenges keep us interested, growing, and alive. When a problem presents itself, look at all the facets. Most problems have multiple veins of crisis, and usually, there is more than one solution. Figuring out how to prevent a problem from reoccurring is an opportunity in itself. Solving the problem provides opportunity for an optimistic view, as well as confidence for further successes.

When you look to praise instead of criticize, you are taking accountability for your emotions and your thought processes. It is much easier to find what's wrong than it is to find what's right in any given situation.

Consider this. Would you be more willing to strive harder in the future to repeat an opportunity for praise when someone you cared for noticed something you did right, or something you've improved on? Or would receiving criticism be more of a motivator?

Personally, I (and I believe, most people) enjoy having a compliment now and then and try to repeat the action(s) that brought the compliment or praise in the first place.

When reading the six definitions I wrote for being optimistic, number four says having an aura that's relaxed and friendly is an important part of being optimistic. If you think about it, you'll realize it's hard to remain optimistic when you're stressed, uptight, or cranky.

Having an optimistic expectation sets you up for success. It sets you up to be pleased. If you start your day with negative thoughts, you'll see the haze of imperfection, the fog of indecisiveness, the lull of motivation. Yuck! Why do that to yourself?

See the possibilities. Envision success. Be the person others enjoy being around. How? How can you be the person others enjoy being around if you don't see yourself as lively, interesting, or communicative?

Make it your mission. Most people like to interact with others (at least for short periods of time on a daily basis.) I bet you do too. Think about the people you enjoy being around. I bet they are the happy ones, the ones that don't dwell on the negative.

Sure, bad things happen, and mean people cross our path, but let it go. Out of every action is an opportunity for you to choose to find the good in it. Sometimes, it is easier to let ill will go than others, but even on big errors it's still possible to let go of the "ill". Sometimes, all it boils down to is the realization no one is perfect and no one has a perfect life.

You've given yourself permission to seek your dreams and goals when you have an optimistic viewpoint.   Dreaming, believing, and visualizing are based on an optimistic attitude. Being an optimist allows you to see the possibilities of success in reaching your dreams – thus helping them to come true.

O.R. Melling writes in *The Book of Dreams* (Amulet Books, 2009), "Against the vagaries of fate and suffering, we have only our dreams and hopes to bolster us."   Hope is the offspring of optimism. If you have no optimism, it is a difficult task to hope and dream.

Maybe your situation is such that your outlook is bleak, so you have trouble finding anything to be optimistic about.

I've had a period in my life like that. I was in a situation because I was being nice, because I was helping out a friend. Towards the end, I sat there one day bawling me eyes out because I couldn't figure how I got myself into this situation, and I didn't see a ready-made solution.

When I went through that period in my life, I searched for what was good about me, and what was good in me. Leaving (running away from) the situation was my only choice. I had to draw upon what little courage I had to realize there was a better place, and that there were options for me. I was optimistic.

It wasn't easy, but in order to overcome the situation, I had to find a new job and a new city far away from where I was. Fighting was not a good option. Once out of the environment, I was able to heal my heart, my ego, build a healthier foundation of self-respect, and find worth in myself.

After leaving that situation, one in which I was used, conned, cheated-on, lied to, and one which showed signs of potential physical abuse because of certain incidents, I realized I had so much more to offer, and I realized I had my daughter's life and safety to consider too.

That was in the early 1990's. After getting out of, and away from the situation I was in, I began to feel optimist about my future. I learned a lot of lessons during that time that won't be repeated.

Write in your Source Book other ways to support an optimistic attitude.

"A candle loses nothing by lighting another candle."
Erin Majors

Responsibility

Dr. Stephen Covey gives an example of responsibility as "the ability to choose a response." When you think about it, you have a choice to how you react to any given situation.

The old saying, "when life gives you lemons, make lemonade," is a perfect example. Another good example is one used by Dr. Covey in a seminar of his. You have plans to attend a picnic, everything is packed, you are excited, and then ... it starts pouring rain.

You can get angry and play the victim because your plans are ruined. Or you can adapt to the situation and have your picnic inside, snuggle in front of a fire, play a game, and enjoy.

How you react to the situation determines whether you are proactive or reactive. Reactive people are victims. Everything is done to them. They accept no responsibility for their life. Proactive people take charge of their dreams and accept responsibility for what happens around them and to them. Who has more control over their life?

How you react to a situation is your choice. You have a responsibility to yourself to abolish your prejudices, your bias, and your preconceived assumptions.

A revealing story tells about a man recently divorced. The divorce was not an amicable one, and final legal documents were expected anytime. A package delivery driver dropped off an envelope, and the man's assistant placed it on his desk.

Throughout the day the man looked at the envelope and glared, growled, and grumbled. Eventually, after hours of anguish over the documents inside, the man rips the tab, and a single document falls out.

Hesitantly, the man picks the document up and begins to read. His face, which had been contorted in anger, rearranges his features to portray a grin from ear to ear.

He had chosen to darken his entire day when he received the delivery. Now, hours after receipt, he learns that his bid for an important project has been accepted.

He could have just as easily received the envelope and chosen to not let it ruin his day. He could have opened it immediately and gotten over the issue. Doom and gloom will find you. Why seek it out?

You have the choice to be positive or negative in every action. I believe everything has a silver lining. Something positive will come. Sometimes, you have to look really hard to find it, and it may not be what you expected, but it's there.

Happiness is your responsibility. Here are a few steps you can take to become happier, fulfilled, decisive, and open to possibilities.

- Develop whatever "gifts" you have to the fullest. Can you (to name a few) paint, dance, sing, teach, preach, or counsel? Using your "Given" talents brings optimism and happiness by channeling the positive energy you into a benefit for yourself and others.
- Take a moment to look at nature. The beauty, the art, the harmony, and the ability to adapt to change bring optimism (and relaxation) to the heart, mind, and soul.
- Dream big, dream small, just dream, dream, dream.
- Be around inspirational people and/or people you respect.
- Be a mentor. Have pride in yourself—your accomplishments multiply as you give to others.
- Identify your fears and take steps to alleviate them. Allow nothing to hold you back.
- Assume full responsibility for your own happiness.

Responsibility is a trait that can be taught and can be learned. It's tedious work on both ends. As a parent, trying to teach my children to be responsible for their actions is like pushing a rope up hill, but eventually threads of the rope snag and gets stuck. It's an exciting day when you watch your child assume responsibility for their action or their mistake, even for picking up their own mess.

Taking responsibility for your own happiness is more difficult than teaching children to accept it, especially if responsibility isn't something you've done too well with in your earlier years.

If you've read anything of my history, you know that I started taking responsibility for my own happiness (and success) about 5-7 years. Why the change? What spurred me to move from my comfort zone—because to accept responsibility for one's own happiness is ***leaving*** one's comfort zone—to start actively setting goals and seeking my dreams?

One occasion was when I was driving on the freeway doing my vocal eases (conditioning for my vocal cords—something I've been doing almost daily for 15 years) and the question came to my mind why? Why do these everyday? Why subject my family to hearing these horrible sounds; because I'm never going to do anything with my voice. With that thought, my eyes started to tear up. I pulled the CD from the player and drove in silence. I thought to myself, I'll just give up. What a relief, no more vocal eases, no more dream of writing hit songs or hearing my songs on the radio.

The void was immediate. The idea of not singing, not writing songs, not writing period. It threw me for a loop. I resolved to do something with my music that very day. About nine months later, my first track for my CD was recorded. *I am responsible for my future and my happiness.*

Write in your Source Book additional ways to become more responsible for your actions and achieving objectives.

You should... You must... You need to...
You ought to... You have to...

How often have you said these phrases to yourself?
How often has someone said them to you?

Responsibility destroys "I have to." In its place is
"I want to, I choose to, I desire to."

Think how much more enjoyment, productivity, and performance you'll get out of doing something you choose to do than something you *have* to do.

7:
Communication

Did you know communication occurs in multiple ways? There is verbal communication which has four distinct styles (aggressive, passive-aggressive, passive, and assertive), non-verbal communication which includes written communication, visual stimulation, body language, and auditory communication, such as music and noise patterns.

Each style or manner of communication is open to interpretation, bias, and misunderstanding. Each style or manner of communication is also influenced for both the sender and receiver due to cultural differences and traditions.

When viewing communication as a foundational quality to a healthy, positive, beautiful you, you'll want to identify your style and what "words and ideas" you project. *Surprisingly, non-verbal communication is received in as little as 4 seconds!*

This means you have projected communication by the way you stand, the manner in which you sit, whether you give eye contact or avoid it, the type and style of clothing you wear, the styling of your hair, the jewelry you wear, and the tone of your makeup. Everything on your person communicates something about you.

Read the verbal communication style descriptions to see which one fits your method of delivery best.

Aggressive: The aggressive communicator takes no responsibility for her actions. When the aggressive communicator talks she uses words, such as "you and your," as in "This wouldn't have happened if you had done what I told you to do," or "It's your fault the sun didn't come up today!"

Having a conversation with an aggressive person is exhausting. You never know when they are going to throw a zinger at you. *"We wouldn't be in debt, if you made more money."* The other person is always at fault. "He made me drop it! She told me to do it!"

Where the aggressive communicator causes anger and resentment, the passive-aggressive communicator causes confusion and withdrawal.

A **passive-aggressive** communicator may say "yes" and commit to doing something, but she never had any intention of living up to that commitment! She says yes, but purposely does not follow through. It's her way to say, "Here you go, now suffer." Usually, the things the passive-aggressive communicator doesn't follow through on or complete is important, maybe even critical.

A good example is the wife who was entrusted to pick up a very important suit from the cleaners but "forgot," or the daughter that promises to pick something up on her way home and doesn't, or the special meal that was burned "on accident," these are all passive-aggressive communications.

Have you, or someone you know, had a difference of opinion but didn't admit it? Then shortly thereafter you accidentally slam the cupboard door while putting the dishes away, or the bathroom/bedroom door slams innocently on just a touch.

The third style of verbal communication is the **passive** style. A passive communicator is one that lets everything slide off her back. She'll take on the job of PTA president, car pool coordinator, shuffle her schedule to accommodate your changes, make a seven-course dinner at a moments notice, and lie across muddy potholes so you can walk on her back and not get your shoes wet.

But inside, the passive communicator is hurting, and she doesn't know. Sure, she thinks, she does a lot, but you're worth it. Yes, she agrees, working from sun up to sun down without rest puts a strain on the mind and body. And no, she really doesn't need a vacation or a kind word. She is doing what she was made for. Serving, she says, is her calling in life.

As my friend Marla put it when we were discussing this communication style, "her ultimate payback is death. She has everyone dependent on her and *now what will they do?*" They should have appreciated her.

An assertive communicator speaks what is on her mind when the issue arises. When a person speaks assertively, she says what the problem is without placing unnecessary blame, and she does it without theatrics or grandstanding. The assertive communicator doesn't communicate in excessive emotional outbursts either.

Sure, the assertive communicator can have passion for her subject. Yes, she can also communicate excitedly with her hands.

What the assertive communicator doesn't do is start a statement with "you." "You have to punch in." "You dropped the ball and the company's going down!" Instead, the assertive communicator would say: "Punch in when you start work." "Because of the missing report, the company will lose the account." That isn't to say there aren't times when someone isn't at fault. The assertive communicator is able to counsel and correct without inflicting verbal abuse.

 Which type of verbal communicator are you?

7:2 Becoming Assertive

The healthiest communication style is assertive. Although some societies are collectivist in culture (the United States is an individualist society), stating your wants, needs, intentions, and desires in a straight-forward manner need not be antagonist, insulting, or culturally taboo. It is possible to maintain a collectivist nature (meaning doing what is best for the group instead of the individual) and still be assertive. Assertiveness is talking in a manner which gets your point or need(s) across instead of avoiding the situation or conversation.

For those who would like to become less of one style and more of the assertive style, here are a few verbal and non-verbal communication techniques you can use.

1. Introduce yourself first. This shows your confidence, even if you're faking it. It also puts the other person at ease. If you've met before, remind the other person of your name and how you met.

2. Seek to understand before trying to get your point across. I read this in Dr. Covey's book *The 7 Habits of Highly Effective Families.* It makes fabulous sense. You show value to the ideas of others when you listen wholeheartedly and strive to understand what they are trying to say.

3. When conversing, restate what is being said to ensure understanding. So many times a task must be repeated due

to a misunderstanding. Often, a remark made innocently offends the receiver. They misunderstood the intent.

When writing, ensure the correct message has been crafted before you send it out. It's so easy to misunderstand. "I picked him up with one arm." Did I pick him up by his arm, or did I pick him up with one of my arms?

4. Take 100% responsibility for understanding the other person's point **and** for getting your point across. It serves no purpose to blame the receiver because they didn't understand the message. Find another delivery method.

5. Listen without interrupting. Your turn to talk will come. This technique is so difficult. You're not only supposed to wait to tell them what is on the tip of your tongue, you are supposed to be actively listening, not formulating a response.

6. Children deserve to be heard. Give them respect, and they will learn to respect others too. I raised my daughter to have an opinion but to also to respect the opinions of others as well. It is a beautiful feeling when adults tell me how much they enjoyed speaking with her. She can articulate, state her opinion, and formulate educated guesses.

Sometimes I want to put a clothespin on **MY** lips when I'm talking with my son, so I don't interrupt him. He's 13, and it takes an hour and a lot of false starts to get to what he wanted to talk about in the first place. So far, I haven't given into the temptation of the clothespin, but when I slip and cut him off mid-sentence, you can be sure he lets me know.

7. Avoid communicating with your arms folded across your chest or your hands on your hips. This is a defensive and aggressive style of communication.

8. Wringing your hands when talking or listening causes you to appear nervous or insecure.

9. Sit or stand straight, with your shoulders back, your hands

placed at your sides or on your lap. This exudes confidence, etiquette, and approachableness.

10. It may seem off-track, but look your best at all times. You have more confidence when you look your best. Your posture is better, you're more willing to talk, and you aren't self-conscious. Plus, when you "look the part" you expect people to treat you as if there weren't a question to your authority.

7:3 Command of Anger

Marla Stone, LCSW, coined "Anger Command," and I use it here with her permission. When angry or upset, remember to speak your feelings without jumping on an emotional rollercoaster. Start with the basics: I feel (insert adjective) about/when (insert the action or event causing the problem) and I (insert validation.)

Let's say the following happened. You are on a lunch break and sitting with some co-workers. Your boss comes up and starts criticizing your work on a project. How would that make you feel? How would you react to such an intrusion? Well, you can yell back, or you can use Marla's Anger Command.

An example would be to assertively confront your boss (in private) by calmly saying, "Boss, I felt humiliated when you criticized me in front of my peers. I understand how you may have thought it was not my best work, or that I didn't follow the given instructions. I am sorry. I will ensure I understand what is expected next time. "

You *may* have given your best work, but it still didn't measure up because you were going by what you *thought* was correct. You know, we never know what we don't know.

It would be detrimental to the Anger Command process to tell the boss that she didn't provide good enough instructions. The best solution is to take the extra minute and clarify expectations before beginning the task. That will alleviate any confusion, and you'll save time in the long run.

If your boss listened to what you had to say and believed you, she may validate in return. If, on the other hand your track record isn't too good, she may not believe or validate you. The purpose of Anger Command is not what SHE will or won't do. It is about you and how you assert yourself.

It is important to let others know how YOU feel, and for you to express yourself in a calm, respectful manner, and then validate the other person's feelings.

Validation Examples

- I know you've considered all the avenues and you'll make the right choice.
- I love you.
- I respect your decisions.
- I'm sure you'll work through it. You always do.
- I think you're so smart. I know you'll get it next time. Remember how well you fixed a similar problem?
- You have high standards. I will work to meet them.

Without ranting, raving, name-calling, put-downs, long discussions, whining, crying, yelling, or quivering. Just validate the person and acknowledge the discussion.

7:4 Descriptive Adjectives

On the next couple pages, you'll find some examples of adjectives to use. You'll want to choose an adjective that gives the exact meaning, or as close as possible to what you want to say.

Adjectives you can use in "Anger Command"

abandoned	adequate	adored
affectionate	affective	afraid

Adjectives you can use in "Anger Command"

alert	alienated	alive
amazed	amused	angry
annoyed	antagonistic	anticipating
anxious	apathetic	appealing
apprehensive	appropriate	ashamed
attractive	awed	bad
baffled	bashful	benevolent
bewildered	bitter	bored
brilliant	cared-for	caring
comfortable	concerned	confused
consoled	content	courageous
curious	cynical	degraded
dejected	delighted	dependent
despised	disconsolate	discontented
discouraged	disdainful	disgusted
dismal	dismayed	disturbed
eager	edgy	elated
embarrassed	empathic	enchanted
enraged	enthusiastic	envious
esteemed	estranged	excited
exhausted	fatigued	fed-up
fond	forlorn	friendly
frightened	frustrated	furious
futile	glad	gloomy
grateful	gratified	great
guilty	happy	hateful
helpless	horrified	humiliated
hurt	idolized	impatient
important	impotent	indifferent
indignant	ineffectual	infatuated
infuriated	insecure	intelligent
involved	jolly	joyful
jubilant	lethargic	liked
listless	loathed	lonely

More adjectives to help you say what you mean

loved	lustful	miserable
mixed-up	moody	nervous
optimistic	panicky	passionate
peaceful	perplexed	popular
proud	provoked	puzzled
regretful	rejected	relieved
repulsed	repulsed	resentful
resigned	respected	satisfied
scared	self-conscious	shocked
shy	sick	smart
strong	sullen	superior
supported	sure	suspicious
tempted	tender	tense
terrified	threatened	tired
torn-up	tranquil	troubled
trusted	trusting	turned-down
unfulfilled	unhappy	unloved
unpopular	upset	useless
valiant	vengeful	vibrant
wanted	weak	wearied
worn-out	worried	worthy
zealous		

How you say something is almost as important as what you say. What your body language is saying can be contradicting what your words are saying.

Effective communication occurs when you: 1) Use the appropriate tone of voice. 2) Choose your words carefully. 3) Ensure your body language is saying what you want it to say.

In your Source Book, write down any other adjectives you can think of to help describe and communicate your true thoughts and feelings.

"If you think you can or can't, either way you're right."

Henry Ford

Do you want it?

You have the potential, now make the opportunity.

8:
Potential

A truism: You can only perform to your self-devised limits.

You have probably heard someone say, "You can be anything you want to be," or "You can do anything you want to do if you put your mind to it."

Both of those statements are partially true, and I have said both to my children. Yet, they are incomplete statements without the backup foundation of some really important adjectives, adverbs, and nouns.

You can be anything you want to be if you have *a positive self-image*, are *motivated*, know your *self-worth*, see your *potential*, set *goals*, have the *self-discipline* to do the steps necessary to reach those goals, take *responsibility* for your actions and feelings, and maintain an *optimistic* outlook during the rough times.

In this book, we have discussed or will discuss each of those foundational qualities. We started with self-image and discussed what a negative or positive image will do for you.

Next we discussed motivation. After learning methods to keep motivated, we found D.A.R.C.I.E. Remember DARCIE, the ingredients for self-worth? We discussed the powerful qualities of optimism, responsibility, and effective communication.

Why didn't we discuss potential first? We didn't discuss potential first because you must first have a strong foundation to build upon before discussing your options.

- A positive self-image is the most important foundational quality you can possess.
- Staying motivated is critical to affecting change.
- Accepting yourself, respecting yourself, having confidence in who you are today and finding yourself deserving of who you want to be must all have a strong foothold on your conscience if you want to even seriously consider your overall potential.

Is potential the same thing as goals? No. Will potential get you there, where ever "there" is? No, not without possessing the other foundational qualities outlined, dissected, and discussed in this book. Everybody has potential for or in something. Not everyone has the desire, the motivation, the self-worth, and everything else needed to get them where they want to go.

One thing is clear though: potential is an individual quality. Your potential comes from natural talent, inherited genes, early environment, knowledge, and opportunity.

Opportunity affects potential, but primarily in the early childhood years. Much of it you make yourself. When you reach 8, 9, and 10 years of age, you consciously make choices. The choices you make affect your potential. This is truer and more substantial every year thereafter.

I'll give you an example. Let's say a healthy child was born into a low-income family. Many people say this child, by age

5, had already lost potential and is disadvantaged. True, some advantages may have been lost for early intervention and development if the environment was not stimulating and supportive of learning.

On the pretense that the parents are loving, supportive, and to the extent possible, involved with their child as the child becomes a student, there isn't any reason this child could not expand his potential by expanding his education. Trying different things, reading about different things, and watching different types of educational movies and videos all expand a person's potential if it causes an interest or desire.

One way to look at potential is to realize how important education is to the process. *You don't know what you don't know. Potential doesn't make itself known until it's called upon.* Opportunity plays into this, but before opportunity comes knowledge.

Here is where the choice comes in. A child, a teen, and adult choose to learn about things. They choose to expand their knowledge by:
- Reading
- Participating
- Watching
- Listening
- Having the desire to know more

Another example is natural ability. You can have natural ability for something but your body isn't going to shout out, "Hey, I have this natural ability to hit a golf ball 360 yards, shoot a basketball from the three-point line, or dance as a prima ballerina."

It isn't until the interest or desire is there and you *try* to do something that you find out you have natural ability, that you have the *potential* to do something with this natural ability. Of course, what you do with both is up to you. Living up to your potential is: Using your environment to the fullest means...

- Living life (family, professional and social)
- Taking care of yourself in the best way
- Using your mind to capacity
- Staying motivated, excited, and optimistic

Ask yourself these questions:

- Do you wake up happy to be alive?
- Do you see each day as the potential it is to get you one step closer to your goal?
- Can you honestly say you loved, cherished, and shared those feelings with your family today from the get-go?
- Have you exercised your mind and body today at its potential?
- Are you eating right, not smoking, not drinking excessively, and balancing your time with what is important to you and your significant others?
- Do you see the opportunity instead of the fear of change?

8:2 Increasing Potential

Once you *find* you have potential in something, or *want* potential in something, you can increase your potential by:

- Doing only what is true and honest. Keep your integrity.
- Reading a wide variety of literature. By doing so you'll gain insights into things previously unknown or misunderstood.
- Realizing fear of the unknown will always hold you back. You become more aware and less afraid by reading and experiencing new things.
- Increasing your energy level. Eating right and exercising. Potential is affected by motivation which is affected by energy.
- Becoming open-minded. Seek others' opinion to a variety of matters.

- Identifying your three best and worst qualities. Focus on the positive.
- Thinking positive, goal-oriented thoughts. Keep negative thoughts from creeping into your mind.
- Trying to see yourself as others see you. Would you want you for a spouse, employer, or employee? Is there a key issue holding you back?
- Asking for feedback. When someone sees your potential, find out what they see and thank them for their feedback.
- Becoming committed to something you believe in. When you practice commitment, you learn to see potential in a new, encouraging light.
- Believing in your potential. Your track-record with following through or completing something you have committed to helps your self and others believe in your potential.
- Working toward achieving your potential realistically. Visualize a gradual influx of life-changing qualities and habits, not an over-night binge of exorcising the bad habits and negativities. Discontinue risky behaviors immediately, but use moderation and common sense on expectations in the area of thoughts, language, and other learned behaviors. Quitting bad habits like cussing, smoking, drinking, unhealthy food, hours of television, and web chatting in one night is a recipe for failure.
- Respecting your self enough to be honest. You have the potential to do a great many things. Honestly assess what it is you want to do or improve.

What can you do today or this week to increase your potential? Write ideas in your Source Book.

Additional Notes

9
Discipline

When one thinks of discipline, punishment may come to mind. The root word of discipline is to learn, not to punish. It is training, self-control, and methods done repeatedly to produce a result. It is those classes, exercises, and lessons taken to build a foundation for a healthy, happy you.

Have you noticed how difficult it is to say a kind word, smile meaningful, or do a good deed, when you feel lousy or are dissatisfied with something in your life?

Realistically, you can only do good things if you feel good, but you can make anything happen if you are disciplined and want something bad enough. Discipline is such a powerful quality to have, and it is behaviors learned. Tips to become more disciplined:

- Repetition of healthy habits. These are habits that bring you closer to who or what you want to be. Nothing in these habits wastes your time or limits your thinking.
- Nudge along your good habits and watch as your dream shapes or materializes toward completion. Celebrate each milestone.

- Visualize the results every day. When you can see it happen, smell the victory, feel the adrenaline surge, then you can remain focused on achievement. The Beauty Seminars Dream Mask is a plus for this visualization time.

Do you believe discipline is the difference between failure and success? If yes, good for you. If not, think about how the Olympic swimmers get to the Olympics, or the cross-county skier makes it across the trail. It is the daily practice, the come hell or high water, the doing-what-you-have-to-so-you-get-what-you-want philosophy. Going to work or school, exercising, doing chores, these are also examples of practicing discipline.

Discipline affects your health, your body, your attitude, your family, everything that affects your life. Celebrate your assets and improve your liabilities. Follow these four key points to improve your discipline: 1) Prepare. Gather all needed resources. 2) Learn. 3) Practice. 4.) Stay motivated.

Preparing to become disciplined isn't much different than the planning process at work. Instead of a mission statement, you're making a statement of intent for yourself.

Instead of deciphering your organization's cultural identity, you're identifying the necessary (maybe even critical) changes to your identity. Learn how changing or stopping that habit can benefit you. Knowledge is power.

Once you've collected all your resources and learned the ins and outs of what you intend to change, make the change.

You can practice by visualizing the intended outcome, making positive posters of what you want to achieve, or by making your acceptance speech. It's important to keep the intended success in the forefront of your day and of your mind. This is how you can stay motivated. For each step along the way—make sure you notice the minor accomplishments along with the major ones.

10:
Goals

"You need to have a goal." Has someone ever told you that? What if you didn't know how to set your goal? What type of goal should you have? How big of a goal should you have?

What is a goal anyway? It's an end-point. Something you want to accomplish as a final result or end product of your effort. It's your payoff.

Goal-setting isn't just a catch-phase. It is the cornerstone of the foundational qualities of a happy, healthy, positive YOU!

Goals become your action plan when you add commitment. If you set your goals too low—like to get through the day, to get through the week—you set yourself to reach just that, and then you're exhausted. That's all you can do.

This is called self-limiting beliefs. You can only achieve what you think you can achieve. That's why it is important to be around positive, supportive people when you are trying to change. Being around unsupportive people who tell you that you can't do something limits or makes you question your belief in yourself, making it very difficult to stay on course.

Also, realize that it takes the same amount of energy for a successful day as it does for an unsuccessful day. You can have a wonderful life with the same amount of energy as a horrible life.

Goals are a common thread that runs between goal-setting, motivation, potential, optimism, self-discipline and self-image. Together, these qualities help build your foundation for a healthy, positive you. It's important to know the "rules" of goal-setting, the whole package that makes change a success. These rules are:

- Goals must be achievable
- Goals must have a purpose, a "why"
- Goals require self-direction and commitment
- Goals must be specific and measurable, but can change
- Goals can be piggy-backed (objectives and milestones)

Before you can set a goal, you have to know what you want, and you have to believe you can achieve it. If you have not been in a position to discover what you want, *realize what it is you don't want and work from there.*

Goals are personal and aren't based upon the wishes or dreams of another person or persons (example: you *should* become a doctor because it's expected, even though you dislike the sight of blood).

Your goals are a reflection of what is important to you and are in concert with your why. They are worthwhile, yet challenging enough to bring a sense of accomplishment. They fit in with your other goals aren't detached or unachievable "nice to have goals" (like a goal to hike on a mountain, but you're afraid of heights, don't hike, and don't like the outdoors).

120

Your goals have a deadline or end date. Someday, maybe tomorrow, or in a few years doesn't make a tangible goal. When you think about it, it's best to make staggered goals.

Types of Goals
(Think: Stepping Stones)

1. Immediate: Now, this week
2. Short term: Within 1 to 3 months
3. A program or campaign: 2–3 months or over the summer
4. 6 months
5. 1 year
6. 5 years
7. Retirement

Try setting more than one type of goal. For example, you can have an immediate goal, a short term, one that's a year out, 5 years, and of course, retirement. Your goals, once set, are as permanent as pencil. As you grow as a person, your goals will probably change. Try the ideas on the following pages to set some personal goals.

Read through these goal-setting techniques, and then after you've thought about them, complete the pages in your Source Book. Keep a pencil handy to jot down some ideas as you go along.

- What are your dreams? Your *real* dreams? When you lie down at bedtime or (hopefully) *during your dream time,* what is it that brings a smile to your lips or a sense of completeness to your soul as you visualize what it is you truly want?
- What do you need to learn (skills, education, licenses) for your dream? Is there something in particular that is an ingredient that requires outside sources?
- When do you want to reach your goal? What is your time-frame? Immediate, short term, 6 months?
- What are possible obstacles to completing your goal?

- Is there anything you need to put-aside or give up so you can concentrate on your goal?
- What will happen (the consequence) if you don't complete or reach this goal? Are you willing to accept that? If not, continue on with the steps.
- Now, break your goal down into steps (like syllables in a word.) First, write *I will*, and then *I'll*....

Remember goals are achieved one step at a time. The steps should be far enough out (a week, month) to be challenging, yet not so far out that you get lost or distracted, or worse, forget what your goal is. Steps toward the goal should be measurable. You measure the success of a completed step by defining, in advance, what is successful. For example, measuring a milestone midway, to ensure I maintain my goal to lose 10 pounds in 3 months would look like this:

- *First, weigh-in at beginning of goal-setting. Record it. My midway point of the goal completion date is 6 weeks. So, at 3 weeks, I weigh-in to measure my success so far.*
- *Then, if I am making progress, which would be 5 pounds lost, then I'd continue doing what I was doing. It was working.*
- *Next, if at my pre-mid-point weigh-in I find I have only lost 3 pounds, then I will need to step up my diligence in following my weight-loss program, or adjust the program slightly because I was not responding to it in a manner I'd meet my goal.*

It's important when setting goals to be sure and...

- Acknowledge **and** celebrate each successful step completion.
- Monitor your progress. Readjust when you go off course.
- Realize that goals may change and other avenues open up as you learn and grow.

Putting it all together

Self-esteem, confidence, self-worth, positive image, dreams, and goals are all part of the makeup of the inner you. You have to have a dream for a dream to come true.

Remember that people with specific goals fueled by desire are able to achieve success because they focus on that desire and that goal. What specific goal will you set for yourself?

And lastly, without a goal you wander or sleepwalk aimlessly through life. You may not realize until you take the time to think about it, that there really is something you'd like to accomplish during your lifetime. If you don't take the time today, it's probable you'll wake up one day wishing you had ...

Allow me to share a story showing how beneficial a road map or plan can be. At a networking event, I met a lady who had a friend that was "stuck." She wasn't sure exactly what to do or how to get there. Her friend went to my goal-setting workshop and learned the steps I've shared with you. Here is her completed goal statement.

Linda's Goal Statement

1. What do I want in the:

Next 6 months: *Get my high school diploma.*

Why do I want this? *I want to finish something.*

Next year: *I want to get a better-paying job.*

Why do I want this? *I want to be able to support my daughter and myself, without help from the county.*

2. What do I want to do in the next 6 months to a year? *I want to go to Community College.*

3. What do I need to learn? *I need to learn how to use a computer and how to write better.*

4. What obstacles might I encounter while working toward my goal? *Money, time constraints, reliable baby sitters.*

5. What are my steps to overcoming my obstacles and reaching my goals?

a. Apply for financial aid.

b. Interview sitters and hire a backup.

c. Attend an adult school that is close and has classes that I can fit into my schedule.

d. Study enough so I feel confident in passing the test.

e. After getting my high school diploma, enroll in a community college.

f. See a counselor at school to make sure I am on the right path and doing the right forms.

g. Find classes that interest me, but that also lead to helping me earn more money.

h. Don't give up.

6. Who can help me accomplish my goal (either by providing guidance or assisting me in overcoming obstacles?) *The county may have job assistance programs and guidance, the school may offer reliable childcare on a sliding scale, there might be not-for-profit organizations that can provide financial help.*

Open your Source Book and think about your own goals and how you can complete a goal statement.

"If a blade of grass can grow in a concrete walk and a fig tree in the side of a mountain cliff, a human being empowered with an invincible faith can survive all odds the world can throw against his tortured soul."
Robert H. Schuller

11:
A Touch of Spirituality
and Forgiveness

This handbook would not be possible without the support of a few friends, nor would this handbook be possible (actually not even conceived) without the internal feeling of there being more to beauty than the makeup you put on your face, the style of your hair, and the clothes you wear.

I have a spiritual center that I draw from. I, of course, do not know your beliefs. I can hope you have a love and a belief in a Higher Power, and that your love brings you peace.

To explain why I bring spirituality into this book, I need to explain that if there is a shimmer of belief inside of you, you need to feed that power to heal completely. But if you *no longer* believe in a spiritual center, a Spiritual Being, or a Higher Power because of the events in your life, you may want to re-look to determine if you do or if you don't carry those beliefs deep down and hidden away.

If you believe your Higher Power, or your spiritual center has forsaken you—until you come to terms with this Spiritual anger—you will not fully heal. Your belief is a part of you. You can't heal 80% and expect to be whole.

I never asked why I wasn't protected from some of the learning points of my life, but I do look back and see that there were always options I could have taken. There was always a fork in the road, and there were always signs warning me of the danger ahead. It was my choice to take the path I had taken, and I accept that. I wouldn't want it any other way.

Some people remark, without those events, there wouldn't be a book. So see, there is another plan for you if you didn't choose the right path first.

I have included my inner most private feelings so I can share an exercise my friend Marla introduced to me. She told me that we are given the answers we need, and that everything we need to know is inside us.

This viewpoint was given after I used the excuse I needed to do more research for this book, instead of just buckling down and writing. When I'd said that, she replied, "What's in those books and articles were other people's thoughts, not yours (as in me)." How could I argue with that?

11:2 Peaceful Journey

This exercise, what I term 'The Peaceful Journey,' is on the CD. I've expanded it and tweaked it a little, but the basic principle of what Marla shared with me is the same.

You have been given you what you need to succeed. To find the answers, you need to ask and listen. Some times you have to wait for the answer. Listen to the CD when you are alone and have some time to devote to yourself.

Below, it is in written form. You'll want to read it all the way through aloud first, and then, get comfortable. Read it a second time with feeling and visualization. Then, close your eyes and concentrate on the visions and sensations you just read. You don't have to remember every detail, because what is important to you will flow from your memory. Also, you may do this exercise many times (never consecutively) and have a different, yet relaxing and rewarding journey each time.

Note. Now is the time to ask a question that the answer, when given, will help you understand, you. It isn't to ask if you're going to be rich, or who loves you, or the numbers for the lottery. It is the time to ask the question you need an answer to.

Some of the more usual questions are:

- Which path to take
- How to ask forgiveness
- How to give forgiveness
- How to be a better "something"

Whatever is pressing on your mind and heart at the time is a valid question.

You will remain seated at all times. During the exercise, you will mentally get up, and mentally walk. After the exercise is complete, you may wish to do a standing stretch, which is recommended.

To prepare for this exercise, sit in a chair or on a couch just enough, so that only your bottom is on the seat. Your hands should be able to dangle freely when not in your lap. Place both feet flat on the ground close together. Place your hands in your lap.

Close your eyes and try to relax, letting all worries go.

Imagine you are sitting on a giant rock outside the forest. The rock is shaped like a comfortable chair and supports your body fully. You run your hands over the rock's smooth surface. As you sit on the rock, you watch as a small rain cloud moves toward the trees and hovers over the forest.

127

As you focus your ears, you can hear the drops of rain as they fall from the sky and land on the leaves in the trees. Softly, the rain caresses the leaf with its moisture. As you focus on the leaf, you can feel the worry and anxiety slip away, releasing the pressure built up in your head. Like the rain washing away the soot of the day, your tension eases.

You feel a smooth warm blanket wrap around your shoulders and realize it is your tension leaving your neck. Drop your chin down, move your head slowly in a circle. Move your head one more time slowly in a circle. Slowly rotate your shoulders up and around to the back, up and around. Let your head fall back and do a slow half circle left and a slow half circle right. With each controlled move, you move stress and worry further from your body. Exhale the air you've been holding and feel the pressure leave your chest and back. Raise your arms slowly up, pushing gently, stretching your arms overhead and then bringing them down around to the sides. Push those negative feelings past your torso and down your legs.

With your hands open, palms face down on your thighs, run your hands down the front of your legs slowly, with a slight amount of pressure under your hands, you lean forward and move your hands all the way down to your ankles. You feel the slight stretch of your back as you move your hands and lean forward. Bringing your hands up the back of your legs, your palms and fingers apply gentle pressure to your calves on the way up your leg and then down again to your ankle. You bring your hands up your calves once more, returning to a normal sitting position, and raise your arms over your head and down to your sides again.

As your feet dangle slightly off the rock, you feel your tension and worry seep out of your feet like a leaky faucet. Slip away, slip away, the tension slips away.

When you are ready, when you are tension free, in your mind, you get up off the rock and stretch appreciatively. Gone are the creaks and uncomfortable strains of everyday life. With a smile on your face, you begin your journey into the forest.

The silence envelopes you as you walk, making your footsteps along the path barely audible. You maintain a healthy pace that is not too fast and not too slow. With awe and gratitude you take in the beauty around you. Your lungs fill and release in a smooth, rhythmic motion as you breathe in and out.

You deeply inhale the fragrance of the blooming flowers without worry. You are not allergic.

You watch the tree's branches sway in the light breeze and realize how perfect the temperature is. You come to the top of a hill and look at the wonder around you.

From the hilltop, you see your destination, a white sandy beach. The waves are breaking gently in the surf. You leave the hilltop and head toward the beach. As you reach the beach, you notice a bearded man off in the distance.

The man is walking towards you. As you begin walking in his direction your heart fills with joy and your mind empties of everything except your question.

When you meet, you sit on the knoll above the water. He turns to you and looks into your face. His glance is like velvet against your skin. Loving, soft, and exhilarating. He seems to say, "Open your heart and open your mind. Ask me your question and listen for the answer without rush, for it will come."

Then he says, "What is it you want to know?"

In your mind, you ask your question and listen for His answer.

129

After you have asked the question, thank Him. Take a deep breath. Exhale. Close your eyes and take another deep breath. Exhale again. When you open your eyes, He is gone.

With the answer to your question tucked into your heart, you begin your journey back through the forest. The tranquility and balance are imprinted in your memory, another gift you can revisit throughout the day as you desire. You smile as you reach the giant rock. You are able to go on about your day with a smile.

Open your eyes. Take a deep breath and let the air exhale slowly.

Use the information you gained wisely, and revisit this fulfilling process, this exercise as needed.

Remember this. When seeking the answer to a question that will make you a more caring, compassionate, and giving person, then that is a good question. To be *those* things, or to have *those* traits, means you must first love the person **you** are. Healing *your* hurts opens your heart to helping others heal as well.

11:3 The Power of Prayer

"Prayer may not change things for you, but it sure changes you for things."

Samuel Shoemaker

If you made changes or put changes in place in your life for the better while reading this book, I salute you! Change is difficult, and it doesn't happen overnight either.

I want to share another idea with you. This idea is forgiveness. I have needed to request forgiveness for things I've done, and I have needed to give forgiveness to others for things they have done to me. Probably everyone has...

I see it this way. If you are learning tools to make changes in your life and getting things straight with whomever you feel spiritual attachment to that comprises 50–80% of your issues.

The rest of it, your need for development, the grungy feeling, the guilt, the anger, and the resentment you may feel—that 20–50% of *you*, well, that has to be addressed before you can fully heal.

11:4 Steps in the Healing Process

Here are the steps I used in my healing process to forgive *myself* and others. Maybe they can help you too.

1. Identifying the root of the problem. I needed to be sure about why I was feeling guilty. What was it I needed forgiveness for? And what had transpired against me that I needed to forgive my aggressor?

2. Pray for guidance.

3. Figure out what you will say to the person involved in the forgiveness process. Approach them humbly and without placing any blame. Seek forgiveness. In almost any transaction there are at least two people. That means it is unlikely only one person is totally at fault. Remember the goal here is to seek forgiveness for your part in whatever transpired, not to re-hash the issue or assign blame.

A key point to asking forgiveness for healing is this. It's not your responsibility to get the "yes, I forgive you."

Your responsibility is to be 100% sincere in your heart that whatever you have done to this person and whatever you have asked forgiveness for, that you are truly sorry for the infraction. That's it.

If they don't forgive you or they place additional or conditional requirements on it (like I'll forgive you if you wash my car), that isn't your responsibility. But it is critical you are 100% sincerely sorry. Healing will not occur if you approach forgiveness flippantly.

4. For those people you are unable to seek forgiveness from in person, through writing, or over the telephone, you will need to ask for help from a Higher Power. Pray with a loving heart, be sincere, and ask for His intervention.

5. Forgiving those who have transgressed against you, especially those that have not asked to be forgiven, takes love and courage.

For you to be able to forgive someone, it is important to think about how the transgression occurred in the first place. It's also important to accept what part (what percent of guilt) you had in it. Once again, it is rare that one person is 100% at fault, unless the action was intentional or malicious.

Once you have realized the issue, and you want to forgive this person, decide whether or not you want to let this person know. Your healing does not require you send any kind of statement that you have forgiven someone of something. In fact, you may open another can of problems by calling up someone and saying, "Just so you know, I forgive you for ruining my favorite dress 5 years ago." You may get an answer different than, "Oh thank you, that has been weighing heavily on my mind."

Sometimes, the one needing forgiving is the self. In my case, I had a few things that I had done wrong earlier in my life, and I knew they were wrong when I was doing the act. Yet, I continued on my course of action. Years later, when I began to heal, when I began to look closely at the actions in my life, I noticed this blanket of guilt I'd been carrying for quite some time. It had smothered me. It was as if when I would do a kindness or a good deed (which was often), my prior guilt was there telling me I was still trash, I was still unworthy of finding true love or goodness. My guilt had crippled me into thinking I would forever be 2nd or 3rd best, unwanted by anyone of substance, and unable to succeed.

It wasn't until I forgave others for the wrongs they did to me that I realized I had to ask my higher Spiritual Being to forgive me, and then I had to forgive myself.

When I was ready to face myself, I chose a time when I knew I'd be alone for some time. I got out a mirror big enough to see my whole face, and I looked deep into my eyes. After a few moments of searching my eyes, I said out loud, "I forgive you for the mistakes and the wrongs you have done. Free your heart." It took a couple times, and a little more prayer and soul searching, but I can say now that the blanket has lifted. When my past is dredged up before my eyes by my dark side, I remind myself it is the past and it has been forgiven by me, and by my Spiritual Being.

It is a wonderful feeling to have a heart free of guilt and anger. Sometimes though, the hurt runs so deep and has been there so long it is like it is a part of us. Try the steps mentioned above, but you may want to consider seeking the help of a licensed counselor.

There is an approach called Transactional Methods and/or the Gestault Method. A counselor can walk you through identifying the issues and help you "face" your tormentor in a safe, fully conscious setting. Marla Stone is a master at helping her clients overcome transgressions occurring decades ago. This method might help you too.

Loving yourself is the beginning of loving others. When you love yourself and accept yourself even with your faults, you'll learn to accept others too.

Notes

12:
When You've Been
Emotionally Hurt

Have you been hurt or intentionally hurt someone? Have you done something that unintentionally hurt another? You probably have. Almost everyone has.

But sometimes a person is hurt so deeply that it causes her to rethink her opinion of herself. Sometimes she can't seem to recover her sense of former self because the hurt is so debilitating. What I'm talking about usually occurs with either the infidelity of a lover, husband, or mate, or losing one's job.

Let's first talk about when our mate cheats on us or leaves us for another woman. It's only natural to lose some self-confidence or have some misgivings about what you have to offer after being betrayed.

Your mate is someone you have given the power to affect your self-confidence and self-worth. Disagree? Do you (or did you) try to look your best for his approval? Were there specific things you did (or didn't do) to please him? Of course there were. That is part of the relationship mix, trying to please or provide pleasure in a multitude of methods.

When our trust is broken, our efforts not deemed good enough (as demonstrated by his actions) or when our sensuality or appearance is devalued, it is going to hurt.

What makes his actions so devastating is that we assume responsibility for our mate's transgression when we allow him to assign us blame. He assigns blame when he says things like:

a. "It's your fault."
b. "You made me do it!"
c. "You weren't...(pick one) "sexy enough, we didn't have sex often enough, you didn't meet my needs, you're frigid, you're boring, you're horrible in bed, you're too fat/thin, your breasts are too big/small, your don't turn me on."

If you have ever been told that (a, b, or c), I relish the fact of informing you that you don't have that power! Even if you are/were the most beautiful or sexiest woman in the world, you don't have the power to keep your man from being untrue.

Plenty of beautiful women, women who are rated as "the sexiest" or "most beautiful" on a number of lists, magazines, and men's sites, are hurt because their husbands cheat.

Infidelity is normally the result of a person's lack of integrity, an effort to prove how appealing they are, denial of responsibility, and/or acceptance of weakness and/or giving into temptation.

Why would you accept responsibility for that?

If you weren't the person having the affair, then you weren't the wrong-doer, or the one lacking in integrity, or the one that allowed desire to overrule basic moral values.

Remember in Chapter Six we talked about responsibility?

It's the ability to choose a response or take an action. When someone blames another for his actions, he is denying his responsibility for his action ... AS IF HE HAD NO CHOICE.

You are making the choice (or have made the choice) to believe you are not worthy, or too thin/fat, or exciting/boring, etc. You are making the choice to assume his guilt by believing his reasons for his actions. To make it even clearer, if I can, when your mate blames *you* for *his* actions, he is asking you to take *his* responsibility of choice away because *he* isn't happy with the results. It is *his* failing, but he blames you.

Everyone has a choice about being true or having an affair. You have a choice in overcoming the hurt or letting his actions ruin your life.

I do have a caveat to add though. As someone who had low self-respect and lacked self-worth when younger, I crossed moral boundaries without thought. I didn't respect my self or my body. I've done things that I'm not proud of now, and for which I've sought forgiveness, but still, many, many years later, the "new" me cringes for some of my past actions and insensitivities.

If you or your mate suffers from a lack of self-respect or feelings of worthlessness, I hope you've read chapters two and four and started working on loving *your* self and respecting your self. It's nearly impossible to respect the moral boundaries of others when you don't possess the foundational qualities of a healthy self-image, or don't set and respect your own boundaries.

I've shared this because it would be difficult to recommend methods of healing—methods I've used when I've been hurt (and yes, cheated on), without including mistakes I've made. I'm still not perfect but I've grown immensely, and now I can set and respect boundaries.

12:2 What can you do to start healing?

First, accept that you can't make someone do something or make someone not do something. If you were blamed for lack of sex, lack of ingenuity, or lack of sex-appeal, communication may have alleviated the "doing-without" feelings he suffered, or it could have helped you feel less inhibited. A MFT (marriage and family therapist) would be the most appropriate mediator to help you get in touch with your feelings and his.

If you don't want sex, is it because of how he makes you feel? This is a trick question, because he can't make you feel something. You choose how to act or react to his words, gestures, or actions. Ask yourself:

- Do you feel desirable?
- Do you find your mate desirable?
- Do you have a mental block to enjoying sex?
- Do you have a physical reason for not enjoying sex?
- Do you enjoy your mate on other levels, such as talking, humor, or common interests?

If you don't feel desirable, you'll be inhibited in your love-making. Inhibitions leave you feeling like you're missing something. It is like having an apple pie without any apples.

You can learn to feel more desirable by learning to accept your body. Imperfections and all. (Chapter 2). You can get in-touch with your body as well (Chapter 13).

Setting and achieving personal goals (Chapter 10), exercising, healthy lifestyle, and finding out what your mate enjoys (and learning to execute the actions) all bring a sense of desirability to our psyche.

On the flip side, if you don't know what your mate likes or aren't pleasing him, this can make you feel undesirable. Once again, communication is the key.

If he left you for a woman that's younger, thinner/bigger, more intelligent/less intelligent, or whatever that is the opposite of you, once again, don't assume his guilt, or his feelings, or his lack of integrity.

Realize you may not be the fit to his everything, or he may not be the fit to your "everything."

Still, it hurts. What can you do?

It is important for you to look within and learn (or reaffirm) who you are, what your values are, and what your dreams and goals are. He may not want to be a part of your future, but it is self-condemning to think you can't live without him.

You can go on. You can examine your self-image (what makes you happy, what would you like to update. Chapter 2). You can examine your goals (do they need updating or a new path. Chapter 10). You can examine what your motivation in life is (is it your man, or your dreams, or a family? Chapter 3).

The biggest mistake you can make when you've been hurt is to succumb to the pain. It is natural to mourn what was lost, what was taken, or what was done to us. Although they are different for each person, there are limits to the length (and depth) of healthy mourning.

Okay, so you were dumped, left, cheated on, lied to, conned, diseased, or suffered any other malady inflicted by another. That's unfortunate, and that's life.

Mourn your loss, wallow momentarily in self-pity, cry at the unfairness of it all ... and move on. You may be financially ruined or bottomed out in the self-esteem level, but if you're alive, you can survive.

Now is the time to re-invent your self. Become the woman you want. Learn a new trade, get healthy or in shape, give up smoking, drinking, gambling, or whatever your crutch.

Sometimes it takes hitting your lowest peak to realize that you'll survive. Sometimes, that awful event that caused you so much pain has a silver lining attached to it, and that silver lining will enable you to become a healthier, happier, more content YOU than you would have been able to achieve without suffering the pain.

And last, I beg you not to assume someone else's guilt or lack of integrity. You may not have been the perfect mate, and you may have acted in a manner that prompted him to action, but it was his action. It was his failing, not your failing.

It hurts my heart to see or hear of women feeling like less of a woman because her man strayed. As I've said before, if he is going to stray, it doesn't matter if you're the sexiest woman in the world. He is going to do what he wants to do to the extent that his conscience can handle.

So let's recap.

1. Cry, mourn, feel sorry for your self for an appropriate period (a day or a week, two weeks.)

2. Discern why he strayed/left. What part of it did you play?

3. Decide if you should have some counseling. I recommend an exploratory session with a counselor you are comfortable with. I am 99% sure it will help in all areas of your life.

4. Take stock of yourself, your dreams, and your goals. Are you living them or working toward them, or are you stagnate?

5. Make a plan to do something each day to better your self and work toward an objective that is part of the larger goal.

6. Make any appropriate decisions on the relationship that started this journey of self-healing and self-motivation. Do not automatically think that separation or divorce is the first or best answer. As in all problems and issues, clear

communication can work wonders.

7. Never allow mean, hurtful, or self-defeating thoughts or words to prey on your heart. If your mate blamed you for his actions, there were probably some pretty ugly comments used by him in the denial of his blame. Do not take those comments to heart.

If there is some validity to your responsibility of contributing factors (e.g., you withheld sex as a punishment or you felt inhibited or uncomfortable or you didn't find him alluring), then I suggest you find out why you felt the things you did. Doing so frees up your mind and your thought process to heal your spirit and move forward in your life.

12:3 Traits and Attractions

Examine the traits your mate has/had. Steer clear of men that have these traits. In fact, steer clear of men and relationships until you have your own life in order, until you feel good about yourself, and until you feel worthy of the best life (and men) have to offer.

If you jump right into another relationship, more than likely this relationship will be based on your insecurities and your low feelings of yourself. You'll be trampled not honored.

Honor yourself and lift yourself up to where you want to be or at least be firmly on the path toward your goals.

Once you start doing things to reach your goals, you'll discover you're a different person: an exciting, attractive woman who knows she deserves to be treated with respect and integrity. When you feel that confidence, you'll exude that confidence, and you'll attract men that appreciate a woman who feels she is worth his attention and worth his effort.

Unlike women, in my opinion, men aren't usually attracted

to someone they have to "fix." A woman, in general, tends to see a man and accept his faults. She then pledges to help him get better, to help him to change. She knows she can help him stop drinking or doing drugs or eat better or exercise more. She, to the detriment of self, will stay with him through the hard times to help him change. A man, again, in general, will see the faults and, unless he is already completely in love with this woman, will walk away. It is not in a man's nature to want to take on the overwhelming task of changing someone. Maybe, it's because he already KNOWS instinctively that, for someone to change, that someone has to WANT to change them self.

So for YOU to attract the type of person you WANT to have (self-reliant, goal-oriented, humorous, caring, compassionate, considerate, healthy, loving), you have to bring some of those good traits to the table as well.

Once again, heal your hurts before seeking another relationship. Find your inner strength, your sense of self-worth, and your confidence. Set and achieve your own goals. Bring your self to a place of harmony. *Love yourself first*, and then, seek to share your wonderful self with another.

If you have suffered the pain (and perceived humiliation) of being cheated on or left for another woman, I pray you heal swiftly and that you are a far better and stronger woman for it.

12:4 Losing Your Job

Another emotional hurt is job loss.

If you lost your job, you may have suffered a devastating blow to your ego. It doesn't matter if losing your job was due to economics (down-sizing, reduction in force or RIF, or product/sales decline) or personalities (change in customer service focus, style, culture, or values/beliefs), or qualifications (change in operating procedures, new technology, new quotas/expectations), it still causes a hit to the ego.

Say you lost your job due to a RIF. It's difficult to grasp you weren't chosen to remain one of the team. What if it was a personality issue? It's difficult to grasp you were released because you no longer "fit" the mold your company designed. And if your qualifications didn't meet the standard, then it's difficult to grasp your skills may be outdated or ineffective.

Losing your job raises some of the same hurts and feelings of inadequacy as losing a mate. How can you use this hurt to your advantage? How can you find the silver lining through the haze of betrayal? Try these methods.

1. Evaluate the reason for losing your job. Do you understand the underlying reason(s) other than the generic reason given?

A. Has your company hired young(er) employees with whom you are not in sync? I am not talking about age discrimination. Generation "X" and "Y" people have different ideals, values, beliefs, and motivators than people born in the 1940s, 50s, and 60s. Not better, not worse, just different.

B. Have you recently undergone a transformation that included the "extreme" to "Be who you really are deep down?" Many companies have an image they want to project to the public. New leadership in the company may mean changes. Your change on the inside might have caused changes on the outside that are no longer consistent with the company's image. Examples include style of dress, facial piercing, tattoos, amount of makeup worn, and hair styles. Some companies expect their employees to portray cutting edge styles and may relieve an employee for failure to maintain the look (my daughter works for a company like this), while other companies may expect a toned-down conservative look.

If the company culture or written policy states otherwise, you may be released (fired) for "expressing yourself." Expressing yourself is not usually one of the benefits of the job, or one that is open for negotiation. I'm not talking about appearance in line with religious guidelines (turbans, beards, jewelry.) However, if this is a deviation from your self, your beliefs, and your appearance from when you were hired, you may not be able to successfully plead your case for exception. Only a lawyer can guide you if this is why you were released.

C. Technology has caused many changes in the workplace, and there are many changes still to come. Re-entering the workplace after a lengthy absence can be difficult because of technological advancements as well. While there may be physical limitations (which is not what I'm talking about) that show up in the new duties, initially, many women aren't prepared for the wide range of skills needed to do the expanded job descriptions placed on them by employers seeking to maximize efficiency while minimizing costs. This includes more than just the technical side of the job. Multi-tasking (which many women may are masters at), 24-hour access, adaption to change, peer-to-peer counseling, professional developmental leadership, are all required skills in many jobs today.

2. Bring your skills and methods up to date.
    A.   Learn how to interact with Generation "X" and "Y" people. In general, find out what motivates them? Discover how their independence, teamwork, interests, focus, and values can benefit you and what your vision is.
    B.   Learn new technology, even if you aren't administrative. You'll want to be able to produce a letter in a crunch.

C.   Attend workshops or read books to learn effective methods of handling stress and change.

3. Except for religious reasons and/or except when specifically requested or required in your job, dress appropriate for your age, and tone your makeup to "the natural look" (see my Beauty Secrets book) to maximize features.

4. Unless you are in your 20s (and then even then following fads is not my advice), restrain from facial piercing, excessive ear piercing, and tattoos. I almost didn't get hired for a job I was well-qualified for because of my wrist tattoo. The director didn't like them, and felt like she was going out on a limb hiring "one of *those* kinds of girls."

5. Choose hobbies that will help alleviate stress.

6. Learn breathing and stretching techniques to use during the day.

7. Become an effective communicator.

8. Align your interests, career, and personality. I recommend Carolyn Kahil's book, *Follow Your True Colors to the Work You Love*.

Once you learn the reason for the job loss, you can use that information to your benefit and grow, re-direct, and re-focus your self and your energy into someone and something you want to be. There are plenty of methods to help you reach your goals, and you can find the right one for you.

Notes

13:
Sexuality and Sensuality

Sexuality is a state of mind. When you feel sexual or sensual, you'll enjoy more, feel more, and be more in-tune with your body's likes and dislikes and wants and needs.

You can be perceived as sexy no matter what your shape, your height, your color, or your weight. Will every person find you sexy? Probably not. There are certain preconceptions in the mind of the beholder that sway what he considers sexy, as well as specific likes and dislikes. But this section is not for him. It is for YOU.

Let us assume you are *not* a model by profession with the "perfect" body, flawless skin, exceptional teeth, and an unquenched sex drive. (Which by the way, an unquenched sex drive can be intimidating to the man that feels he can't satisfy you.) Let's say you are a normal adult woman, who has some areas on your body that you aren't completely happy with. When I look at myself, I see some sag in my breasts, varicose veins, grey hair, generous hips, large, wide feet, and let's not forget to mention the dimples on my backside. If that won't give you a complex, what will?

How then, am I supposed to expose all of these bodily

flaws to my husband and still feel good about myself?

Your sexuality is a state of your mind and should center on your thoughts. Love, appreciation, respect, adoration, and encouragement are helpful on the part of your partner, but they won't always be there, especially in the beginning of a relationship, the birth of a child, cancer, disease, injury, weight gain, weight loss, financial difficulties, and parenting issues. How your day went and how your partner's day went also play a role in the whole "state of mind" thing. When you can gauge how your partner's day went, and then adjust accordingly, you will be able to influence both of your "moods" for the good or for the bad.

How can you learn to feel good about your physical self in a sensual and sexual way? Well, my answers aren't for the faint hearted and may seem difficult to try at first. If you follow the suggestions, your confidence will improve dramatically and will improve your intimacy with your partner. It probably would make you happier too.

These are general tips to feel better about your self. Make sure to do these exercises when you are alone and when you do not expect interruptions. The time of day is not of important, but you do need time to explore, time to feel comfortable, and enough available time so as not to feel rushed. For the first time, do the exercise when you are not stressed, upset, or on your monthly cycle. Ready? Here we go.

1. Acknowledge (out loud) there is not one perfect person (or body) on this earth.

2. Have a photograph taken (of your face) in which you look exceptionally good. Companies that use filters, lighting, unusual clothing, and other trade tricks are adept at making you look softer, sexier, younger, and prettier. Display this photo someplace you will see it everyday.

3. Each day, look at the photo and say audibly, "I am a beautiful lady." Stop any negative thoughts that spring into your mind. Do not let them come to pass.

4. Find something on your body or face (more than one is even better) that you like. Nourish and pamper those places. If you like your teeth, have them professionally cleaned and select the perfect shade of lip color to show them off even more. (See my *Beauty Secrets You Can Use At Home* book for help with that.) If you like your eyes, shape your brows and select eye products that enhance those beautiful eyes. If you have nice legs, then massage them to keep the blood flowing, use lotions that nourish and moisturize, not suffocate them. Try to find something new each week or month to love about your self.

5. Love your body. Even if you aren't where you want to be or have what you want to have. It can always be worse. Be grateful for what you have.

6. Exercise. Find time to exercise daily, even if it is not enough to burn fat or raise your heart rate to a training heart rate. If you are more than 20 pounds over what is considered the "ideal" body weight for you height and age, proceed with caution.

The human body is a miraculous thing, but it is not designed to be stagnant for long periods of time and then explode in cardiovascular maneuvers. Without use, muscles and tendons shrink. It is easy to overdo it when you first begin to exercise, and then you can't walk or bend 2 days later, or worse, you tear or strain a tendon. Ouch!

Exercise will make your skin healthier, and your body will function better too. Here's a personal tip. *When waiting for the microwave, or standing at the copier, I do arms exercises, leg lifts, or something to stretch my body and use time management.*

7. Eat a balanced diet. Water consumption is vitally important to skin maintenance and overall health. Hydrated skin looks better and feels healthier. Fruits and vegetables are important parts of your diet, so don't overlook them.

Some Tips & Techniques

The next couple pages include specific tips and techniques that are designed to put you more in sync with your body. They include touching and getting to know your own skin and self, but they don't discuss or include exploring the pelvic or genital area.

Try doing these techniques when you are alone and not rushed. You may feel some embarrassment if you've never done something like this before, but try to get past that. The body is a beautiful, magnificent creation. Some cultures and some influential people in your life may have you believe otherwise, but what you choose to believe is up to you.

Exercise #1:
A get-to-know-yourself-bath

1. Bundle your hair on your head and secure. You do not want it dangling on your neck.

2. Fill a warm (not hot) bath. For this exercise, do not put bath salts or oils in the water. If possible, place candles on the sink, tub, floor, or toilet cover. Remember, safety first.

3. Play soft music, instrumental, without words. Put the volume just loud enough to where you can barely hear it.

4. With a gentle body wash, cleanse your skin slowly. As you run the wash cloth or scrubby gently over your body, feel the skin. In your mind, visualize the cloth caressing your skin. Visualize your skin the way you want it to look, such as soft, and radiant.

5. With your skin above water, lightly run your fingers over

your skin. The touch should be so light that it is seductive and exciting. Appreciate the skin as it tingles under your touch. Appreciate it, but don't give into the seductive or sexual fantasies that may be playing in your mind. Focus only on your skin and your touch.

6. Run your fingers ever-so-lightly up and down the inside of your forearm and wrist. Feel the excitement. Then move them inside and out on your arm. Have the thumb caress the inside of your wrist while the middle finger runs the length of your forearm.

7. Run your fingers lightly, seductively over your breasts. Notice how the body reacts to the sensitive touch. Appreciate the beautiful skin you have. If there are any scars, ignore them. Focus on the feeling of your fingers and the reaction of your skin. As your nipples harden, explore them. Remember you are only lightly touching and caressing.

8. Move your fingers down to your stomach. The stomach is unbelievably sensitive to a light touch. Do not ignore the feel of you skin, or the way it moves under your touch.

9. Stroke your fingers down to your legs. Caress them, appreciate their strength and ability.

10. After you have run your fingers along your legs and calves, prepare to leave the tub. This is not the time to rub your feet or explore between your legs.

11. Rinse off, and towel lightly.

12. Go to a location and position where you are warm, and where you can sit comfortably. With foot cream or lotion, slowly massage the ointment into your feet. Start with the arch of the foot. Use just enough pressure to feel it, but not so much that your hands tire too quickly. From the arch, using your thumb, rub down to the balls of your feet. This is a part of the foot that takes a lot of abuse. Move your thumb

and fingers down and massage each toe independently, and then together. See what actions you like more than others. Finish your feet by massaging lotion into your heel and ankle. The actions and the touch are different on the foot than they are on other parts of the body, but feet can be very sensual if you are comfortable with them.

The bath exercise is designed to show you how your body is beautiful and receptive to touch. This exercise is not to stimulate yourself to orgasm, but to show you that you can love the body you have.

Sexuality truly is a state of mind. Did you notice how sexy you felt when your body responded to your touch? If you use the same technique on your partner, you will feel their skin react and come alive with your touch.

Exercise #2: Your beautiful face

1. Wash your hands with a soap containing an enjoyable light scent. The scent must not be over-powering.

2. Do not bind your hair.

3. Seat yourself in a comfortable upright chair or lie down.

4. Play soft instrumental music just loud enough to hear.

5. Close your eyes.

6. Start with both hands running through your hair to get it off your forehead.

7. With the second and third fingers on both hands touching just at the point in between your eyes (on your forehead), very, very gently run your two fingers (in opposite directions) along the hairline and down the side of your jaw. Feather your touch off along the bottom ridge of your ears.

8. As you pass your ears, using the tops of your fingers (the side with the nail bed), lightly pass the tops of your fingers

152

over the outside of your ears (both ears simultaneously) and flick your fingers outward toward your hair. Do this movement two or three times.

9. Place the second fingers of both hands (which is actually the middle finger) back to your forehead and lightly circle your eyes simultaneously, and then with both fingers touching, travel up the bridge of your nose, and then down the nose to the point of the nose, down the front of the nose, and around the perimeter (outside edges) of the lips. At no time during this finger travel, have you broken the touch.

10. Still using your middle fingers, run them along your jaw line, around your ears, and across your cheeks.

11. Allow your fingers to lightly run along your facial bones, concentrating on the different sensations your touch can arise.

12. Vary speed and intensity. Allow your fingers to "play piano" ever so lightly.

13. Without any tugging what-so-ever, caress your eyes and eye lids. You may discover that just alternately placing your second and third fingers on your eye lids without any rubbing at all is quite relaxing.

14. End your facial exercise by massaging your scalp with all your fingers and thumbs.

Try this exercise on your partner. It is an amazing gift.

Exercise #3: Moving sensually

If you are not accustomed to dancing, let alone dancing seductively, this may be a tad more difficult at first. But soon, you'll be swaying to the music and feeling more sensual and sexy even when you walk.

1. Find a location that has a mirror where you are able to

153

watch the way your body moves. More than one mirror is ideal.

2. Select music that is very slow with a discernable beat to it. It can be either a male or female singer, but the words need to be positive, if not positively sexy and promising. (My song *I Want You I Do I Do* works well with this exercise.) Avoid music that has a negative feel, talks negatively about women, or has a fast beat.

3. Wear something you enjoy wearing, something you feel is sexy. It doesn't have to be an "outfit" or a complete "anything." I once did this exercise in a see-through "thing" and ballet cover-up, nothing I would wear out in public. (Yes, I do this too.)

4. Have the lighting dimmed, using candles if possible.

5. Turn on the music and close your eyes. Begin by swaying to the music and add hip and arm movement as you see fit. If this is new to you, just closing your eyes and letting the music move you--is a good start.

6. As you get more into the music and let loose your inhibitions, you'll want to move to the music, moving your hips, arms, neck, hands, and body seductively.

7. As you move, fantasize. With your eyes closed, see your beautiful body moving to the music. Visualize moving the way you want to move. Visualize how you want to look. Visualize your partner enjoying the more sensual you.

8. You can move as much or as little as you are comfortable. You can visualize and fantasize while moving your hands over your body.

9. You can explore new moves as well as move your body as seductively as you choose.

10. When the song or songs are finished, allow yourself time

to recover. This exercise is very stimulating both in the mind and in the body. Do not expect to go right out of the room to business as usual.

11. If possible, lay back on your bed or in a chair to allow your senses to finish their play. When you feel you have recovered fully, then move on to the rest of your day.

I don't suggest dancing in front of your partner until you are completely comfortable with yourself and your sexuality. Your sexuality at this point is very fragile. A laugh, or worse a snicker, can damage everything you have just gained.

As I have said from the beginning of this chapter, our sexuality is a state of mind, but it is also our own. Feeling sexual or sensual (they are not the same) is something we can do for our self. Feeling sensual (and sexual) adds to our relationship a spice, another flavor. It is exciting to be comfortable with our partner and with our self.

Voluntary Participation in the "I Want You" Video

When you get comfortable with your sexuality, and are confident dancing sensually, you are welcome to participate in the video compilation for the song, I Want You, I Do, I Do. Submissions, (which must include all the information below) which I expect to accept through September 2010, will have different women dancing (alone), preparing to dance, putting on make-up, doing their hair, etc, to do their "I Want You" dance for their mate, and actually dancing to the song.

Please note, there isn't nudity, sex, or anything vulgar in the video, and please don't send any of that. The video, which I expect to sensual, and of a sexual nature, will celebrate women accepting their body, their sensuality, and the romance of desire.

155

Submission Sheet for the "I Want You, I DO, I Do" Video

High-quality video and screen-shot-like photos will be accepted for compilation of the music video for the above titled song. It is expected that submissions will be accepted until September 2010, extended or cut short as the needs of the video are.

This sheet, a copy of it, or a sheet containing all the information required to accompany any CD/DVD submission. Submissions without the required information will not be accepted.

CD/DVDs become the property of the publisher, and will not be returned or receipt acknowledged. If your submission is accepted, you will be notified. Once accepted, you may not remove your submission. All adults, sizes, and shapes are encouraged.

All people in the video must be at least 18 years old at the time of making the video. NO nudity and NO sex scenes are to be submitted. There is **NO PAY, ROYALITIES, or RIGHTS** given for participation in this video. Please print Release information:

Name: _____
Age at filming: _____ Sex: M   F   Phone: _____
Street: _____ APT _____
City: _____State: _____ Zip: _____
Signature: _____

Name: _____
Age at filming: _____ Sex: M   F   Phone: _____
Street: _____ APT _____
City: _____State: _____ Zip: _____
Signature: _____

Please share how this book has helped you: _____
_____
_____
_____

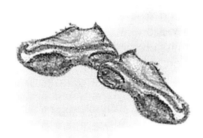

Closing Thoughts

We've discussed many different methods in this book. What has worked for me may not work for you, or you may need to modify the process.

The important thing is start living your life to the fullest. If you're carrying a lot of baggage from incidents, events, and people putting their dissatisfaction or evilness on you, it makes it hard to be free.

You can't be free, healthy, and happy with emotional baggage trailing you. Alice Bernardi, a friend, once said, "People should start out at 60 and work their way down to their 20's."

I agree, except I think it would be better to "live" their way down to their 20s. I wish you the greatest success in finding your dreams, believing you can achieve them, visualizing them, and achieving them.

Comments are welcome, please send them to lorraine@lovingmyselffirst.com.

Re-take the assessment, and just as in the first case, don't think or dwell on the answer to a question. Circle what comes immediately to mind.

1. Do you **often** wish you were **someone** else? **Y N**

2. Do you **often** wish you were thinner or heavier? **Y N**

3. Do you wish to significantly change your appearance as in be taller/shorter, different nose, chin, etc? **Y N**

4. Are you a compulsive volunteer (Can't say no)? **Y N**

5. When praised, do you say "yeah right" or laugh? **Y N**

6. When asked what makes you happy do you have to think about it? **Y N**

7. Is "I'm not sure," your answer when asked about your goals? **Y N**

8. Do you think you have to be outwardly beautiful or rich to get what you want? **Y N**

9. Is being unique or different a bad thing? **Y N**

10. Do you **often** say "I can't, I have to, or I should?" **Y N**

11. Do you make a daily "to-do" list, but still don't seem to complete anything? **Y N**

12. When you make a mistake, do you call yourself a name, such as Dummy, Stupid, or Idiot? **Y N**

13. Do you NOT make a suggestion or NOT try something new because you are afraid to fail or be laughed at? **Y N**

14. Do you believe your mate, a pretty face, or an education is responsible for your happiness? **Y N**

15. If opportunity knocked, would you feel you weren't quite ready? **Y N**

Look for thought-provoking questions on the next page.

If you've read the book and completed the exercises in each chapter, and yet you still answered "yes" to quite a few of the preceding questions, it's important to find out why.

As much as I'd like to think my writing style is captivating and entertaining, this isn't a book to read over a weekend and then put on the shelf.

Just as weight loss and weight gain take time, learning new behaviors takes repetition (at least 21 to 30 days) of doing the same thing every day in the same way.

Changing the way you think can be an epiphany, or it too can take 3–4 weeks (or more) to get it to stick in your head.

So if you think you're too fat or too thin, **_besides exercise and healthy habits_** (like eating and sleeping), the only way you'll get rid of those mind-altering, image-crushing demons is by looking at yourself and telling yourself with clear conviction you're "okay." This doesn't happen overnight. You can't even do it with conviction the first day. Repetition is key. And guess what?

As you're eating healthier, exercising, sleeping right, cutting out the bad things for you (habits, poor-choice-hobbies, drugs, alcohol), you'll notice the positive things happening to your skin, your shape, your hair, your eyes, your lips, and your view of your self. But again, it takes time.

What about compulsive volunteerism or an inability to say no? Even someone from a collectivist society needs time to herself. If you looked at and did the exercises or suggestions in Chapter two (self-image), Chapter four (self-worth), Chapter eight (potential), and Chapter ten (goals), you'd realize you don't have a lot of free time to give away. Volunteering for a worthy cause is a good thing, but that volunteerism can't be at the expense of your health, family, job, or sense of who you are. There has to be balance.

You can get a sense of belonging and a sense of pride when you make a positive difference in other people's lives. It's true. But what if you're the PTA president, volunteer twice a week in your child's class, mentor at church once a week, practice with the choir on Tuesday night, supervise the childcare in church on Sunday, take your child to a sports practice two nights a week, and work a full time job? Don't laugh. It happens. People, good people, allow them selves to get roped into something "because nobody else would do it."

Yet, while every day and night is filled with something for someone else, that book you've dreamt about writing or that dress you've wanted to make or mend sit in the shadows of your mind, unfulfilled and waiting. You miss out on quality family time because you're helping someone else or you can't seem to find the time to relax, read a magazine, or reflect.

Maybe now's not a good time. Maybe you'll wait to fulfill your dreams until the children are out of school, or until there is more money, or until ... Until is like tomorrow. It never comes. 'Cause guess what? Tomorrow *is* today!

Tomorrow you'll sit down and write those first words, and you wake up, and get busy with TODAY. Yesterday is yesterday, always, and it's gone. What did you do with those 24 hours? Did you make something meaningful? Did you take even just a few minutes (more hopefully) and work toward a goal, whatever that goal is? I hope so.

So here's what I'd like you to do. Write down on a 3x5 card, or a lined piece of paper, or get a My Options Reminder (M.O.R.) bracelet, and write down what you want to accomplish, why you want to accomplish it, (by) when you want to accomplish it, and what would happen if you don't accomplish it.

On the back side, write down methods/steps you can use

to work toward that goal. Look at this a couple times a day. Keep it a dominate thought in your mind.

Write down affirmations to repeat every day, 3-5 times a day, preferably, while looking into your eyes in a mirror. Ensure your affirmations are positive, and in the present, such as, "I rock." "I am successful." "I am beautiful."

Use this type of reasoning and reflection when determining why you are stuck on answering "yes."

Realize some days you might answer a question "no," while on other days, it's a "yes." That's okay.

And finally, realize there are plenty of people that can help you overcome the issues you want to overcome. "Want" is the key word here. You must want to be released from self-hate. You must want to see the good in your self. You must want accept that while there may always be parts of you you'd like to be different, you know, yes, *you know* you're alright.

You can be the person you want to be!

Summary

- You can be confident.
- You can be happy.
- You can dream.
- You can set and achieve goals.
- You can change how you perceive yourself.
- You can change how you perceive others.
- You can win over any negativity you received in your past and overcome any obstacle placed in your way, when you DESIRE for this to occur.

Index

Suggested Web Sites

Here are websites and hotlines that could help you become more responsible. They are not endorsed by the author or publisher, just some starting points for you.

Alcoholism
http://alcoholism.about.com/
http://www.mayoclinic.com/health/alcoholism/DS00340

Dieting
http://en.wikipedia.org/wiki/Dieting

Discrimination
http://en.wikipedia.org/wiki/Discrimination#Age_discrimination

Domestic Abuse
http://helpguide.org/mental/domestic_violence_abuse_types_signs_causes_effects.htm
http://www.ndvh.org/ National Domestic Violence Hotline

Mental Health
http://mentalhealth.samhsa.gov/ US Dept Health & Human Svcs
http://mentalhealth.about.com/ another view

Parenting
http://www.parenting.org/ Free advice, tips, & more
http://familydoctor.org/online/famdocen/home/children/parents/behavior/368.html
http://www.usa.gov/Topics/Parents.shtml RESOURCES!

Self-Image
http://en.wikipedia.org/wiki/Self_image definitions and some links

References/Credits

Clinton, H., Secretary of State March 8, 2009, press release, http://www.State.gov/pressreleases

Covey, S. R. *The 7 Habits of Highly Effective Families,* Golden Books, New York, 1997

Gray, P. *Psychology,* Worth Publishing, 1991, 1994, 1999, 2002

Maslow, A. (1943). *A Theory of Human Motivation.* Psychological Review, 50, 370-396. Retrieved August 2008, from http://psychclassics.yorku.ca/Maslow/motivation.htm

Waitley, D., *"Dr. Dennis Waitley Talks About The Ten Qualities Of A Total Winner,"* Nightingale-Conant Corporation, Chicago, IL, 1978

Wilson Solovic, S., *The Girl's Guide to Building a Million-Dollar Business,* Amacom, New York, 2008

Woolfolk, A., *Educational Psychology,* Pearson Education, Inc., 2007, tenth edition

Source Book

The book to use when finding the source of your dreams, ideas, and attitudes. How to use this book:

Copy the pages (cut along the dotted lines) so you can do the exercises and plans now, while you are reading the book.

Some point later in the future, after you've put your plans in action, re-do the exercises to ensure you are on the right path.

When asked to write the first things that come to mind, do it. Dwelling over something skews the results.

Ponder questions only when asked to. Realize that you are the responsible person in charge of your actions.

Remain positive and open to new ideas.

Source Book

My past, my present, and my future are in these pages. [2]

Chapter 2, page 29. What comes immediately to mind when I describe my day:

_____

_____

_____

_____

_____

Chapter 2, page 36. The negative thoughts I have about myself are:

_____

Chapter 2, page 36. The positive thoughts I have about myself are:

_____

Source Book

I am a quality human being.

Chapter 2, page 36. More things I like about my personality and character traits are:

Chapter 2, page 36. Some of my in-between thoughts about myself are:

Chapter 2, page 36. The positive attribute to some of my negative or in-between thoughts are:

Chapter 2, page 38. Some qualities I don't currently possess that I would like to have are:

Source Book

Inside, holds a well of goodness and love.

Chapter 2... It's important to take a moment to appreciate oneself, so below, I will write the things I am happy I've learned or improved thus far...

Dear Me:

Source Book

I am beautiful inside and out.

Chapter 2, page 38. The parts of my physical self I do not like are:

_____

Chapter 2, page 39. Write a letter explaining how the physical dislikes can be changed to likes.
Dear Me:

_____

_____

_____

_____

_____

_____

Chapter 2, page 42. When I get stressed – this is what I think stresses me:

_____

_____

Change is difficult, even when it is good change.

Source Book

Chapter 2, page 42. A closer look at when I get stressed answers these questions:

What time of day is it? _____

Who is involved when I am stressed? _____

What has been going on before I get stressed? _____

_____

_____

Are there any additional reoccurring stress points in my environment I can change?

_____

_____

_____

_____

Source Book

It's important for my health to take some time for me. 7

Chapter 2, My Action Plan to set change in motion is:
1. I want to change: _____

2. I will do this by affirmations: _____
a) _____
b) _____

3. I will use the following tools to help me: _____
a) _____
b) _____

4. If I think a chart of responsibilities is needed, I will draft one right now.

5. I may need to change the way I do things, such as: _____

_____

_____

Source Book

Chapter 3 page 49. What am I motivated in, and what are my motivators?

Chapter 3, page 53. What would I like to be more motivated about?

Chapter 3, page 55. What are my motivating factors today/right now? Realize they change.

Source Book

Every new day is an opportunity.

9

Chapter 3, page 56. What are my desires? I'll visualize my wants and write the details here:

_____

_____

_____

_____

Chapter 4, page 60. Are there any specific things I don't like or accept about myself?

_____

_____

_____

_____

I find something to love about myself daily.

Source Book

Chapter 4, page 61. Ways I can see things about myself differently are:

If my usual thought is:	I can think or do this instead:

Chapter 4, page 61. What thoughts or actions can I learn or adopt to accept ME the way I am today?

Chapter 4, page 64. To be more self-responsible, I may want to improve:

Source Book

I take time to notice the beauty around me.

Chapter 4, page 78. Can I think of any additional keys to confidence? Write them here.

_____

_____

Chapter 4, page 79, Section 4:7, Self-Image questions. Write the answers here.

1. _____

2. _____

3. _____

Chapter 4, page 83. What are other ways to demonstrate my positivity? What actions can I take to reinforce a positive perceived self-image?

_____

_____

I am kind and considerate.

Source Book

Chapter 4, page 86. I disclaim being called a bad name or degrading label. I disclaim it openly and write it here by saying "I am not a…":

_____

Chapter 4, page 90. Here are some affirmations about my growth opportunities, about qualities I would like to improve:

_____

_____

Chapter 4, page 91. Additional ideas I have to strengthen my positive self-worth:?

_____

_____

_____

A sincere kind word immense happiness.

Source Book

Chapter 5, page 96. I can support an optimistic attitude by:

_____

_____

_____

Chapter 6, page 100. Is there some area of responsibility I'd like to become more responsible for?

_____

_____

_____

Source Book

It's a good feeling to find the right words to express my thoughts.

Chapter 7, page 104. What style of communication do I normally use? Is it effective? Does my mood cause me to vacillate between aggressive-passive-passive-assertive? If so, how can I this?

_____

_____

_____

_____

Chapter 7, page 109. What are other adjectives that describe specific or distinct feelings I have?

_____

_____

_____

_____

_____

_____

Source Book

To reach my potential begins with step one.

Chapter 8, page 111. Have I placed limits on myself? Have I put myself into a "final" category? :

Chapter 8, page 115. What can I do to start moving toward or increasing my potential??

Source Book

See http://www.dreamsandgoals.org to view the thoughts and actions of others, and add mine.

Chapter 10, page 121. What are my goals (near and future) and what are my dreams?

_____

_____

_____

_____

Chapter 10, page 122. I will......

_____

_____

_____

_____

Goal Statement

1. What do I want to achieve in the:

a. Next 6 months: _____ Why do I want this? _____

b. Year: _____ Why do I want this? _____

c. Five years: _____ Why do I want this? _____

2. What action/activity do I want to DO in the next 6 months to a year? _____

3. What do I need to learn? _____

4. What obstacles might I encounter while working toward my goal? _____

5. What are my steps to overcoming my obstacles and reaching my goals?

a. _____

b. _____

c. _____

d. _____

6. Who can help me accomplish my goal (either by providing guidance or assisting me in overcoming obstacles?

_____

_____

_____

Make copies of the blank statement and review/update often.

To forgive is divine.

Chapter 11, page 131. Do I need to ask forgiveness, or give forgiveness? If so, why?

_____

_____

_____

Chapter 11, page 131. What steps will work for me in my forgiveness process?

_____

_____

_____

Source Book

Love isn't a weapon, but some wield it as a knife.

Chapter 12, page 135. Is there a hurt I am carrying around that has not healed?

_____

_____

_____

Chapter 12, page 135. Will one or more of the many suggested methods help me heal, if so, which ones, and what is my starting point and timeline?

_____

_____

_____

_____

_____

_____

Quick Order Form

Fax orders: 703.644.5492. Send this form.

Telephone orders: 703-644-5492

Online orders:
www.PoeticExpressionsPublishing.com
or **email** the order—Include the information on this
form and write to: PEPPub@gmail.com

Postal orders-mail to: PEP Publishing
PO Box 2367, Springfield, VA 22152, USA.

Please send the following books or pamphlets:

__ Loving Myself First $18.95 U.S. $24.95 Canada

__ Makeup, Skincare, and More (1st Ed.) $25.50 U.S.

Other publications: _____
_____

Please send FREE information on:
____ Speaking/Seminars ____ Other Products

Name: _____
Address: _____
City: _____ State: ___ Zip: _____
Phone: _____
Email: _____
Shipping: Please enclose $4.00 U.S. or $9.00 International.
Virginia residents also include 5% sales tax.

About the Author

As the daughter of a man who's been married 7 times, and a mom who's been married 3 times, and both of whom were involved in relationships with married people, it's no mystery where a lack of boundaries and an inability to trust stemmed from in my life.

Although not discussed in this POSITIVE and UPLIFTING book, I have been the recipient of the attention of pedophiles, kidnapped, gang-raped, conned out of over thirty thousand dollars, verbally, physically, and emotionally abused, and other horrible learning points in my life. . . . it is surviving those experiences and more that this book and the methods of overcoming life's obstacles (past, present, and future) are based upon.

I mention these experiences only to show that one can survive. Yes, we may falter or we may stagnate for a while, but hopes and dreams will re-surface and seek fulfillment.

I hope this book helps you find the strength or the courage to go after your dreams and to set your goals. The methods work; I am proof of that.

About the Artist/Illustrator

John Mutch was born in Charlottetown, Prince Edward Island, Canada. He has shown his work in several art shows, and over the years he's worked in a broad range of mediums, mostly watercolours and sculpting.

In the last 10 years, he has focused his efforts more on sculpting, but always seems to find a way back to his pencils and watercolours.

He lives with his wife and three children in Moncton, New Brunswick, Canada.

John and Lorraine "met" discussing Brandon Drury's upcoming book on www.recordingreview.com. Both are writing music in addition to the other things in their life.